LAKE GARDA

TRAVEL GUIDE 2025

Essential & Practical Tips to Know Before You Visits this Beautiful Destination

Jillian j. Miller

Introduction

Introduction

Lake Garda is Italy's largest freshwater lake, with a millennia-long history. Its development, sculpted by natural forces and the passage of time, has resulted in a unique setting that has drawn human settlement for ages.

Glacial origins

The narrative of Lake Garda began millions of years ago, during the Quaternary epoch. As glaciers cut their way across the Alps, they left a massive depression that eventually became the lake basin. Over time, the glaciers receded, leaving behind a breathtaking scene of mountains, valleys, and the crystal-clear waters of Lake Garda.

Human History

Bronze Age and Beyond: Petroglyphs discovered in several areas around Lake Garda provide evidence of human occupancy dating back to the Bronze Age.

Roman Era: The Romans understood the lake's strategic value, constructing colonies and expanding agriculture.

During the Medieval Period, the area was ruled by a succession of rulers, including the Lombards,

Franks, and Austrians, each of whom left their stamp on the region's culture and architecture.

Modern Era: The nineteenth century saw great growth, with the introduction of tourism and the construction of large homes.

A Haven of Relaxation and Adventure

Lake Garda is becoming a popular destination for tourists from all over the world. Its magnificent natural beauty, historical charm, and numerous activities make it the perfect destination to unwind, explore, and build wonderful memories.

Chapter 1:

A Brief Overview of Lake Garda

This guide is your all-around companion for experiencing the spectacular and diverse region of Lake Garda, Italy's largest and most picturesque lake. Whether you're coming for the first time or returning to explore more of its charms, this guide will offer you with everything you need to make your trip memorable.

What's in the Guide:

What's New for 2025: Discover the most recent additions and upgrades to Lake Garda, including new cultural displays, eco-friendly ferries, enlarged hiking routes, and gastronomic innovations. We've emphasized everything that makes 2025 such an interesting year to visit.

Detailed Planning Resources: We have provided all of the necessary information to help you plan your trip with ease. From the best times to visit and how to get there to financial advice and what to bring, this guide will help you plan for every part of your trip.

Top Attractions and Activities: Lake Garda is full with natural beauty, historical sites, and outdoor experiences. This book includes all of the must-see locations, whether you want to see medieval castles, hike in the mountains, or enjoy watersports on the lake.

Gastronomic Highlights: Lake Garda has a vibrant and diversified gastronomic scene. We've produced a list of the greatest local cuisine to taste, the finest restaurants, and the most attractive lakeside cafés. You will also learn about the region's wine pathways and innovative farm-to-table eating experiences.

Cultural Etiquette and Local Insights: To enhance your trip experience, this guide explains local traditions, social etiquette, and key regulations. Whether you want to learn how to speak the language or about sustainable travel habits, we have you covered.

Practical Travel Guidance: From navigating public transit to budgeting and avoiding crowds, our practical tips area has plenty of guidance to help you make the most of your trip. We've also included sample itineraries to accommodate various trip lengths and interests.

Why visit Lake Garda in 2025?
Lake Garda is a location where natural beauty, historical significance, and modern conveniences coexist together. In 2025, the region will bring various additional attractions and events, making it even more desirable to visitors. Lake Garda has something for everyone, whether they are drawn to the gorgeous villages, cultural richness, or gastronomic pleasures.

This book aspires to be more than simply a compilation of travel information; it's a carefully chosen resource that will inspire and support you at every stage of your adventure. With thorough information, insider ideas, and practical guidance, you'll be well-prepared to explore Lake Garda and make experiences that last a lifetime.

Set out on your 2025 Lake Garda journey with confidence, knowing that this book includes all the insider tips and information you'll need to make the most of your stay. Prepare to explore the charm of Lake Garda!

Why visit Lake Garda

This book is intended to be your ideal travel companion, whether you are planning your first trip to Lake Garda or returning to discover more of its splendor. Lake Garda, Italy's largest and most stunning lake, captivates visitors with its natural beauty, picturesque cities, rich history, and dynamic culture. From the charming settlements along the beach to the stunning mountain views that enclose the lake, there is something for every sort of visitor.

What You'll Find in This Guide

Comprehensive Planning Tips: Whether you're staying for a weekend or a week, this guide will help you organize your vacation efficiently. You'll discover information on the best times to visit, how to get there, and what to pack, so you're ready for every step of your adventure.

Top Attractions and Activities: Discover the must-see sites and activities that make Lake Garda such a popular trip. We've covered all of the biggest attractions, from medieval castles and Roman ruins to climbing the picturesque trails of Monte Baldo and enjoying lakeside watersports.

Culinary Delights: Lake Garda is more than simply a visual feast; it is also a foodie's delight. The book provides a handpicked selection of must-try local foods, as well as recommendations for the finest venues to eat them. Whether you're dining at a lakeside trattoria or drinking wine in a vineyard, this area will whet your taste for regional cuisine.

Cultural Insights: Understanding local traditions and manners can improve your trip experience. This handbook covers Lake Garda's cultural standards, including language, clothing rules, and social etiquette. We also highlight key legislation and regulations that travelers should be aware of.

Practical Travel Advice: To help you confidently travel Lake Garda, we've included practical suggestions on transit, safety, money management, and more. This area will ensure a smooth and pleasurable journey, whether you need guidance on hiring a car or where to discover the greatest perspectives.

Sample Itineraries: Don't know where to start? Our suggested itineraries will help you get the most out of your time at Lake Garda. These itineraries, ranging from a fast weekend break to a full week of exploration, are tailored to different travel types and interests.

Historical Significance of Lake Garda
Lake Garda has a rich and intriguing history dating back millennia. Its strategic position and natural beauty have made it a desirable place for many civilizations.

Prehistory to Roman Times

Early settlements: Evidence implies that human presence around Lake Garda dates back to the Bronze Age.

Roman Conquest: The territory was conquered by the Romans and became part of the affluent Cisalpine Gaul. The Romans had a considerable impact on the region, with traces of their homes and infrastructure still visible today. Sirmione, in particular, is well-known for its Roman remains, which include the famed Catullus Grotto.

Middle Ages and Beyond.

Lombard and Frankish Rule: Following the collapse of the Roman Empire, the territory was ruled by the Lombards, then the Franks.

Scaliger Dominance: The strong Della Scala family emerged in the 13th century and left an indelible mark on the region's architecture. Their magnificent castles may still be seen in towns like as Sirmione and Malcesine.

Venetian Influence: Venetian authority over Lake Garda began in the 15th century, bringing prosperity and cultural interchange.

Austrian and Napoleonic Wars: The area was a battleground throughout the Napoleonic Wars and the Italian Wars of Independence, with major engagements taking place near Solferino and Custoza.

Modern Era

Tourism Boom: During the late nineteenth and early twentieth century, Lake Garda became a renowned tourist destination. Grand hotels and elegant villas were constructed to accommodate an increasing number of guests.

World War II: The lake region was impacted by the war, yet it retained much of its attractiveness.

Geography and Climate of Lake Garda

Geography

Lake Garda, Italy's biggest lake, is a breathtaking natural beauty tucked in the foothills of the Alps. Its unusual trumpet-like form spans three regions: Lombardy, Veneto, and Trentino-Alto Adige.

Northern Part: Characterized by rugged, hilly terrain that provides stunning views and opportunity for outdoor activities.

The southern part: Has mild slopes, olive trees, and vineyards, resulting in a more relaxing and Mediterranean feel.

Climate

Lake Garda has a distinct microclimate generated by its location between the Alps and the Po Valley. This creates a comfortable atmosphere throughout the year.

Mild Winters: Temperatures seldom fall below freezing, making it a popular winter getaway for people looking for a warmer environment.
Warm Summers: The lake's moderating impact assures pleasant temperatures, ideal for outdoor activities.
Mediterranean Influence: The southern half of the lake has a more Mediterranean climate, with higher temperatures and longer sunny days.

The neighboring mountains shield the lake from harsh weather, resulting in a protected habitat.

Entry Requirements and Visa Information for Lake Garda

Disclaimer: While I give broad information, it is critical to verify the most recent rules before your travel. Visa requirements sometimes vary, so check official government websites or your embassy for the most up-to-date information.

Entry Requirements for EU Citizens:

If you are an EU citizen, all you need is a valid passport or national identity card to enter Italy and visit Lake Garda.

Entry Requirements for Non-EU Citizens: Visa requirements for travelers from outside the EU vary depending on their nationality.

Check Visa Requirements: To discover whether you require a visa, go to the official website of the Italian Embassy or Consulate in your country.

Passport Validity: Make sure your passport is valid for the full period of your stay in Italy.

Travel Insurance: It is strongly advised to have travel insurance that covers medical expenditures.

Additional Tips:

Health Insurance: While not required for EU nationals, travel insurance is generally recommended.

The Euro is the official currency of Italy.

Vaccines: Confirm whether any vaccines are required for your travel.

Passport and Visa Copies: It is a good idea to make duplicates of your passport and visa in case they are lost or stolen.

Remember to consult the official government websites for the most current and up-to-date information on entrance requirements and visa laws.

Chapter 2:

Planning Your Visit

Seasonal Highlights:
Lake Garda provides a distinct experience all year, with each season bringing its own beauty and activities.

Spring (April – May)
Nature's Awakening: The lake and surrounding surroundings are alive with beautiful flowers and lush foliage.
Mild Weather: This is ideal for outdoor activities such as hiking, cycling, and boating vacations.
Fewer Crowds: Enjoy a more tranquil atmosphere compared to peak season.

Summer (June–August)
Sunny Days: There are ideal for swimming, sunbathing, and water activities.
Vibrant Atmosphere: Busy towns and beaches.
Peak Season: Expect increased crowds and pricing.

Autumn (September-October)

Golden Foliage: The environment changes into a stunning array of hues.

Pleasant Weather: This is ideal for wine tasting, seeing attractive villages, and participating in outdoor sports.

Harvest Season: Enjoy the region's delectable food and local vegetables.

Winter (November to March)

Quiet Retreat: Get away from the throng and enjoy a tranquil environment.

Christmas Markets: Discover the romance of the festive season in little communities.

Winter Sports: Visit local mountain locations to ski and snowboard.

Weather and Climate Considerations for Lake Garda

Lake Garda has a distinct microclimate, shaped by its location between the Alps and the Po Valley. This creates a comfortable atmosphere throughout the year.

General Climate

Winters are Pleasant: The temperatures seldom dropping below freezing, making it a popular winter resort for visitors seeking a warmer environment.

Warm Summers: The lake's moderating impact assures pleasant temperatures, ideal for outdoor activities.

Mediterranean Influence: The southern half of the lake has a more Mediterranean climaPackingh higher temperatures and longer sunny days.

Local Winds

There are two primary winds that affect the Lake Garda area:

Peler: A northerly wind that generally blows in the morning and is great for sailing and windsurfing.

Ora: A southerly wind that blows throughout the afternoon, bringing a pleasant breeze.

Packing Tips:

Spring and Autumn: Pack layers because temperatures might fluctuate throughout the day. For the nights, a lightweight jacket is advised.

Summer: Pack lightweight clothing, swimsuits, and sunscreen.

Winter: If you want to explore the mountains, bring warm gear such as a jacket, hat, and gloves.

Water Temperature:

- The lake's water temperature fluctuates with the season and location.
- In general, July and August have the hottest water.

- Because of its depth and proximity to the mountains, the northern portion of the lake is often colder.

Understanding the local weather trends allows you to plan your activities and maximize your stay in Lake Garda.

Budgeting Your Trip

Accommodation Costs on Lake Garda

Lake Garda has a variety of hotel alternatives to suit every budget and inclination. Here's a general breakdown of costs:

Luxury Accommodations

Luxury Accommodations: Are often located in great locations with beautiful lake views.

Luxury Amenities: Include private pools, spas, gourmet restaurants, and butler service.

Cost: Expect much higher rates than alternative solutions. Prices might range from €300 to €1000 or more each night, depending on the season and the house.

Mid-range accommodations are typically located in major tourist locations or lovely villages.

Facilities: Comfortable rooms with minimal facilities, and breakfast is frequently included.

Cost: Prices normally range between €100 and €250 per night, depending on the season and location.

Budget accommodations are typically located in calmer regions or away from the lake.

Amenities: Include basic rooms with communal or private bathrooms.

Cost: Prices start about €50 per night, with hostels providing considerably lower rates.

Please keep in mind that these are only rough estimates, and costs might vary greatly based on the property, season, and booking time. It is best to reserve accommodations well in advance, especially during peak season.

Transportation:

Lake Garda provides a range of transportation alternatives for seeing its breathtaking shores and lovely villages.

Public Transportation: Buses connect most villages surrounding the lake. It's an inexpensive way to explore.

Ferry: Enjoy gorgeous vistas as you cruise between lakeside towns. Ferry service is offered throughout the warmer months.

Train: While trains mostly serve the southern section of the lake, they might be a convenient choice for lengthy trips.

Rental Car

Renting a car provides the most freedom. It enables you to explore at your own leisure and visit isolated locations. However, be prepared for traffic and parking issues in famous tourist destinations.

Bicycle Rental

Renting a bike allows you to explore the lake at your leisure. Many municipalities provide bike rentals, and there are designated riding trails along the beach.

Other Options:

Taxis are convenient yet costly, especially for long trips. Walking is ideal for seeing tiny communities and enjoying the lake's atmosphere.

Packing Tips

Essential Travel Gear & Clothing Recommendations for Lake Garda

The best packing list for Lake Garda depends on the time of year you travel. However, some necessities are necessary regardless of season.

Pack layered clothing to prepare for uncertain weather. Consider a light jacket or sweater.

Swimwear: Required for enjoying the lake's pleasant waters.

Comfortable Footwear: Walking shoes are good for touring towns and trekking.

Evening Wear: While Lake Garda is largely informal, you may wish to dress up for some restaurants or events.

Gear

Sunscreen: Essential for protecting your skin from the sun.

Sunglasses: Keep your eyes safe from the intense Italian sun.

Hat: A wide-brimmed hat is ideal for sun protection.

Insect repellent: Particularly effective in the nights.

Camera: To capture the breathtaking sight.

Reusable Water Bottle: Stay hydrated while helping the environment.

Beach towels are essential for resting by the lake.

Specific recommendations. Based on the season

Spring/Autumn: Pack a light jacket or sweater because temperatures might fluctuate.

Summer: Pack light, breathable clothing, swimsuits, and a cap.

Winter: If you want to explore the mountains, bring warm gear such as a jacket, hat, and gloves.

Health and Safety

Emergency Contacts and Local Healthcare Services in Lake Garda

Emergency Numbers

European emergency number: 112 (functions in most European nations).

The Italian emergency number: 112.

Local Healthcare Services

While Lake Garda is typically safe, it's important to know where to get medical help if necessary.

Note: Healthcare systems can differ by area. It is recommended to have comprehensive travel insurance that includes medical coverage.

Local Hospitals and Clinics: Check with your hotel or the local tourist information center to find the nearest healthcare facility.

Pharmacies: Pharmacies (farmacie) are prevalent and offer over-the-counter drugs. Look for a green cross sign.

Important Considerations:

Language Barrier: Learn basic Italian words for medical situations.

Travel Insurance: Make sure your coverage covers medical bills.

Emergency contacts: Keep a list of emergency contacts, such as your embassy or consulate.

Medication: Bring any essential drugs with you and have a prescription.

Disclaimer: This is a general guide. It is critical to confirm facts before to your journey, as healthcare services and emergency numbers may change.

Safety Tips for Tourists in Lake Garda

Lake Garda is a typically safe site, but you must take care to ensure a worry-free holiday.

General Safety Tips.

Be aware of your surroundings: Be mindful of your surroundings and trust your intuition.

Avoid Strolling Alone at Night: Stick to well-lit locations and consider taking a cab for late-night excursions.

Protect Your Belongings: Keep your valuables safe, utilize money belts or secret pockets, and avoid showing big sums of cash.

Use ATMs in Safe locations: Choose ATMs that are within banks or well-lit places.

Beware of scams: Common scams include counterfeit ticket vendors, overcharging for products or services, and pickpocketing.

Respect the local norms and laws: When visiting holy places, dress modestly and respect local traditions.

Stay hydrated: Drink plenty of water, particularly in hot weather.

Water Safety

Swimming: Stay mindful of water currents and depth, especially in new regions.

Water sports: Always use suitable safety gear and follow professional recommendations.

Boating: Follow boating legislation and safety requirements.

Hiking and Outdoor Activities.

Inform Someone of Your Plans: Share your trekking route and planned return time.

Wear Appropriate Footwear: Choose durable shoes with a good grip.

Carry the Essentials: Pack water, food, a map, and a first-aid kit.

Be aware of weather conditions: Check the weather forecast before setting out.

Additional Tips:

Learn Some Fundamental Italian Phrases: Knowing a few key words can be useful in an emergency.

Bring a Copy of Your Passport and Travel Insurance: Keep duplicates in a separate location from the originals.

Register Your Journey with Your Embassy or Consulate: This might be useful in case of an emergency.

Following these tips will allow you to enjoy your trip to Lake Garda with peace of mind.

Chapter 3:

Exploring Lake Garda's Attractions

Sirmione: A Blend of History and Wellness.

Sirmione, a beautiful peninsula protruding into Lake Garda, is a veritable treasure trove of ancient attractions and soothing hot springs. This beautiful village combines historical beauty with contemporary health.

Historic Sites
1. Catullus' Grottoes.

Historical significance: The enormous Roman villa complex is one of Italy's most magnificent archeological monuments. It is said to have belonged to the Roman poet Catullus.

Rules: Respect the historical site by staying on authorized trails and without touching the remains. Photography is normally permitted, but check for special limitations.

There is an entry fee to see the Grottoes.

2) Scaliger Castle:

Historical significance: This old castle dominates the skyline and serves as a symbol of Sirmione. It has majestic towers and provides panoramic views of the lake.

Rules: Follow the castle's opening hours and any other particular rules supplied by the authorities.

Cost: There is an entry fee for visiting the castle.

Thermal Springs

Sirmione is known for its medicinal thermal waters. There are various thermal spas that provide a variety of treatments and wellness experiences:

Terme Virgilio: This spa in Colombare has a range of thermal pools, saunas, and wellness services.

Terme Catullo: Located in the historic center, this spa offers a magnificent experience with breathtaking lake views.

Aquaria Thermal SPA: This spa offers health and beauty treatments that combine thermal water with current technology.

General Rules For Thermal Spas:

- Follow spa etiquette, such as donning swimwear and showering before entering the pool.
- Respect other visitors by being calm and avoiding interruptions.
- Follow any instructions for using spa facilities, such as sauna and steam room etiquette.

Cost: Prices vary according to the spa, services, and packages selected. Check the official websites for the most up-to-date information.

Additional Tips:
- To save money, consider purchasing a ticket that includes both the Catullus Grottoes and the Scaliger Castle.
- It is advisable to book spa treatments ahead of time, especially during high seasons.
- Take advantage of Sirmione's lovely streets to enjoy local food and shopping.

Explore Sirmione's historical attractions and enjoy the revitalizing advantages of its hot springs to create unique memories of your vacation.

Malcesine: Cable Car to Monte Baldo.

The cable car ride to Monte Baldo offers an amazing experience. Ascending almost 1700 meters above sea level will reward you with stunning panoramic views of Lake Garda and the surrounding Alps.

The Experience
The cable car ride is separated into two halves. The first takes you from Malcesine to San Michele, an intermediate stop. The second segment, known for its

revolving cabins, provides a 360-degree perspective as you climb to the peak of Monte Baldo.

Rules and Regulations

Weather Conditions: Adverse weather can have an impact on cable car operations. Before your travel, check the weather forecast and plan for any potential delays or closures.

Capacity limits: There may be limits on the number of people per cabin, particularly during busy hours.

Safety Guidelines: Wear seatbelts and keep your items secure. Follow the safety advice issued by the cable car workers.

Photography: Take beautiful shots, but be cautious of other passengers and avoid blocking their view.

Respect Nature: Monte Baldo is a protected area, so please be respectful of the environment and wildlife.

Cost

The price of a cable car ticket varies according to the time of year, age, and whether you buy a round-trip or one-way ticket. To get the most up-to-date price information, visit the official website.

Additional Tips:

- Consider getting a combo ticket that allows you to visit other nearby sites.
- Dress comfortably and appropriately for the alpine climate.

- Bring sunscreen, sunglasses, and a hat, particularly on sunny days.
- Pack a picnic or dine at one of the highland eateries.
- Explore the many hiking paths and see the breathtaking environment.

The cable car to Monte Baldo provides a wonderful experience for people of all ages. With careful planning and obedience to the guidelines, you'll have unforgettable recollections of this spectacular excursion.

Limone del Garda: A Taste of Citrus Culture

Limone sul Garda, located on the western coast of Lake Garda, is a lovely village known for its lemon groves. This gorgeous resort provides tourists with a unique opportunity to immerse themselves in the world of citrus.

Exploring the lemon groves

While there are no set "rules" for wandering the lemon trees, it is critical to be courteous of local farmers and their land.

Respect Private Property: Many lemon groves are privately owned. Admire the groves from public places or approved walking trails.

Stay On Recognized Trails: If there are official walking pathways through the groves, follow them to prevent damage crops.

Photography: Take stunning shots of the lemon orchards, but be respectful of people's privacy.

Lemon-themed experiences

Limone Provides a Range of Lemon-themed Experiences:

Lemon-based products: Discover a variety of lemon-based items, such as liqueurs, jams, oils, and cosmetics.

Lemon-infused cuisine: From pasta to desserts, enjoy wonderful meals made with fresh lemons.

Lemon Grove Tours: Some local enterprises provide guided tours of lemon groves, which provide insight into the farming process.

Lemon-themed Activities: Keep an eye out for festivals and events that honor the town's citrus legacy.

Costs

Product Purchases: The cost of lemon-based items varies per item.

Guided Excursions: Prices for lemon grove tours vary based on the tour operator.

Dining: You may enjoy lemon-infused meals at typical restaurant pricing.

Additional Tips:

Best time to visit: Spring is the best time to see the lemon groves in full bloom.

Photography: The golden hour, just before sunset, is an ideal moment to photograph the splendor of the lemon trees.

Local Delicacies: Try the wonderful "Limoncello," a lemon-flavored liqueur that embodies the essence of Limone.

Limone sul Garda provides a pleasant getaway for both nature enthusiasts and foodies. Immerse yourself in the town's citrus culture and make wonderful experiences.

Riva del Garda: Where Adventure Meets Relaxation.

Riva del Garda, located on Lake Garda's northern side, provides the ideal balance of thrilling activity and peaceful leisure.

Adventure Activities

Riva del Garda is a paradise for adventure seekers:

Windsurfing and Kitesurfing: The lake's high winds make it a popular site for these water sports.

Rock Climbing and Hiking: The surrounding mountains provide numerous options for climbers and hikers of all skill levels.

Mountain Biking: Discover gorgeous routes and experience the excitement of downhill riding.

Paragliding and hang gliding: Take to the sky to enjoy beautiful views of the lake and mountains.

Rules & Regulations:
- Follow safety requirements and wear suitable equipment for all activities.
- Respect nature and do not harm wildlife.
- Obtain the appropriate permissions or licenses for specific activities like climbing or paragliding.
- Check the weather before going outside.

Costs:
- Rentals and instruction for water activities, climbing, and riding.
- Lift passes for mountain riding.
- Tandem flights for paragliding and hang gliding.

Relaxation and Leisure

After an adrenaline-packed day, relax and rejuvenate:

Lakefront Promenade: Take leisurely strolls or bike rides along the lovely waterfront.

Beach Relaxation: Bask in the sun on sandy beaches or grassy grounds.

Boat Tours: Explore the lake by boat and take in the breathtaking views.

Shopping: Visit local boutiques and stores that sell one-of-a-kind items.

Dining: Enjoy fresh seafood and local cuisine at the seaside eateries.

Rules & Regulations:
- Respect public areas and don't trash.
- Follow any local beach rules, such as sunbed rentals and forbidden objects.
- When spending time on the lakeside, keep other guests in mind.

Costs:
- Tickets for boat tours.
- Food and beverages in restaurants and cafés.
- Shopping expenditures.

Riva del Garda provides something for everyone. Whether you choose action or leisure, this dynamic town will provide you with amazing moments.

Natural Wonders and Outdoor Escapes

The Dolomites and Monte Baldo:
The Dolomites

The Dolomites, a UNESCO World Heritage Site, are a mountain range in northeastern Italy known for its spectacular peaks, verdant valleys, and crystal clear lakes.

- Activities include hiking, climbing, skiing, snowboarding, mountain biking, and simply admiring the breathtaking surroundings.
- **Rules:** Follow defined routes, respect animals, and stay alert of weather conditions. Always take necessary supplies like as water, maps, and a first-aid kit.
- Costs include lodging, transportation, lift passes (for skiing), equipment rentals, and guided excursions.

Monte Baldo.

Monte Baldo, sometimes known as the "Garden of Italy," is a mountain range that overlooks Lake Garda. It has a wide choice of activities and breathtaking vistas.

- Activities include hiking, bicycling, paragliding, cable car trips, botanical gardens, and leisure.
- **Rules:** Respect nature, stick to established routes, and obey cable car laws. Keep an eye on the weather, especially if you plan to do anything outside.
- Costs include cable car tickets, equipment rentals (bikes, paragliding gear), guided excursions, and botanical garden admission fees.

Combining the Two

Many travelers combine their stay to Lake Garda with a visit to the Dolomites. This provides a variety experience, ranging from resting by the lake to strenuous alpine experiences.

Transit: While renting a car allows you greater freedom, public transit is also available.

Accommodation: There are several alternatives available, including hotels, apartments, and mountain huts.

Planning: Determine the optimal time to travel depending on your favorite activities. Summer is best for hiking and riding, while winter is good for skiing and snowboarding.

Important Considerations:
- During peak season, both the Dolomites and Monte Baldo may get busy, so plan your lodgings and activities ahead of time.
- Before you start any outside activity, check the weather forecast.
- Prepare for altitude sickness, especially while climbing at higher heights.
- Respect the local norms and traditions.

By carefully organizing your itinerary, you may fully immerse yourself in the natural splendor of these two renowned places.

Parco Giardino Sigurtà, a botanical wonderland.

Parco Giardino Sigurtà is a vast botanical garden in Valeggio sul Mincio, near Lake Garda. It's a must-see for nature enthusiasts, because to its spectacular flower displays, different landscapes, and peaceful environment.

Rules and Regulations

Respect For Nature: Visitors are urged to be respectful of the park's plants and animals. Picking flowers, harming plants, or disturbing wildlife is strictly banned.

Stay on Authorized Pathways: To protect the delicate environment, visitors must stick to the indicated trails and avoid going across lawns or sensitive areas.

Picnics: While picnics is permitted in specific places, trash is prohibited. Always dispose of rubbish correctly.

Photography: While photography is normally permitted, the use of drones or other flying devices is forbidden.

Animals: Pets are normally not permitted in the park.

Costs

Admission to Parco Giardino Sigurtà costs vary according on season, age, and extra services (e.g., guided tours or bike rentals). To get the most up-to-date price information, visit the official website.

Additional Tips:

Best Time to Visit: The park is most gorgeous in the spring, when the flowers are in full bloom.

Comfortable Shoes: You will be walking a lot, so wear comfortable shoes.

Camera: Remember to bring your camera to capture the beautiful views.

Bike Rental: Renting a bike allows you to explore the park at your leisure.

Guided Tours: Consider joining a guided tour to learn more about the park's history and floral wonders.

Parco Giardino Sigurtà provides an amazing experience by allowing guests to immerse themselves in nature's splendor. By adhering to the park's laws and regulations, you may help conserve this valuable refuge for future generations.

Varone Falls: A Natural Spectacle

The Varone Waterfalls are a breathtaking natural phenomenon near Lake Garda. This spectacular cascade plunges into a steep valley, producing an unforgettable scene.

Rules and Regulations

Safety First: Follow all safety warnings and directions. Wear suitable footwear since the location may be slick.

Stay on approved trails: To safeguard the natural environment, please follow the defined paths.

Photography: Take beautiful shots, but be cautious of other guests and avoid using flash photography, which may disrupt the natural light.

Respect Nature: Don't trash or damage the local flora and wildlife.

Costs

There is an entry charge for the Varone Waterfalls Park. The price covers entry into both the top and lower caverns, as well as the surrounding park area.

Additional Tips:

Waterproof Attire: While not required, wearing waterproof gear might improve your experience, particularly if you visit on a wet day.

Camera: Remember to bring your camera to capture the breathtaking splendor of the waterfalls.

Comfortable Shoes: With adequate traction are recommended because the terrain may be uneven.

Combine With Other Activities: The Varone Waterfalls are readily connected with a trip to Lake Garda or other surrounding sites.

Varone Waterfalls provide a unique and wonderful experience. Follow the regulations and respect the natural environment to properly appreciate this natural treasure.

Chapter 4:

Activities and Experiences

Hiking and Biking around Lake Garda

Lake Garda is an outdoor enthusiast's heaven, with a wealth of hiking and riding paths suitable for all fitness levels. Here are some of the best paths to explore.

Hiking Trails: Monte Baldo offers stunning panoramic vistas and is a hiker's heaven. The trails range from simple to difficult, accommodating to all levels.

Tremalzo Mountain: Located in the northern section of the lake, provides breathtaking alpine landscapes and pleasant excursions.

Ledro Valley: This calm valley has a number of hiking routes, including those through forests, meadows, and along the lakeshore.

Bardolino Hills: These hills are ideal for a leisurely trek, with mild slopes and picturesque olive trees.

Biking Trails

Limone sul Garda: Known for its citrus plantations, Limone has lovely bike lanes around the lake and across the countryside.

Riva del Garda: This dynamic town is the starting point for a variety of bike paths, ranging from simple to difficult.

Gardone Riviera: Take a leisurely bike ride along the lakeside promenade, or venture into the hills for a more strenuous adventure.

Monte Baldo: For skilled mountain bikers, the descent from Monte Baldo is an exciting challenge.

Important Considerations:

Trail Difficulty: Before going on a walk or bike trip, research the trail's difficulty.

Equipment: Make sure you have the right gear, such as comfortable shoes, a map, and enough water.

Safety: Tell someone about your intentions, especially for longer treks or bike journeys.

Weather: Before going out, check the weather forecast, as conditions in hilly places can change quickly.

path etiquette: Respect other hikers and bikers and observe path rules.

Additional Tips:

Consider taking a guided walk or bike trip to learn about the area's history.

Bike Rentals: Many communities surrounding Lake Garda provide bike rentals for both standard and electric bikes.

Maps: Buy comprehensive maps of the region to assist you navigate the trails.

Picnic: Bring a picnic lunch to enjoy on your walk or bike ride.

Explore the numerous hiking and bike routes surrounding Lake Garda to find breathtaking scenery, fresh air, and amazing experiences.

A World of Water Sports:

While sailing, windsurfing, and kayaking are great water activities, there are plenty of other exciting choices to try. Let's delve in:

Powerful Water Sports

Wakeboarding: This is a sport that involves riding a board while being dragged behind a boat and executing tricks and leaps.

Waterskiing: This is a classic water activity in which two skis are dragged behind a boat.

Jet Skiing: This is the practice of riding a personal watercraft at high speeds with enthusiasm.

Flyboarding: A jet-powered board that allows you to hover above the water and do airborne moves.

Underwater Adventures

Scuba Diving: Using scuba gear, explore the undersea environment and find beautiful marine life.

Snorkeling: Enjoy the underwater splendor with only a mask, fins, and snorkel.

Free Diving: Diving underwater without a breathing equipment and depending on breath-holding skills.

Surfing and Boardsports

- Surfing involves riding ocean waves on a surfboard.
- Bodyboarding is the practice of lying on a tiny board and riding waves.
- Paddleboarding (SUP) is the practice of standing on a surfboard and using a long oar to paddle.

Other Water-based Fun

- Whitewater rafting involves navigating tumultuous rivers in an inflatable raft.
- Rafting is similar to whitewater rafting, but on calmer water.
- Canoeing is the activity of paddling a canoe, which is commonly used to explore lakes and rivers.
- Tubing is when you relax on an inner tube while being dragged behind a boat.

Paragliding: Soaring above Lake Garda

Paragliding over Lake Garda provides an unforgettable experience, enabling you to take in the breathtaking splendor of the lake and surrounding mountains from above.

Best Places For Paragliding
Monte Baldo: The most popular launch spot, with stunning vistas and steady wind conditions.
Monte Pizzocco: A less-crowded option with breathtaking surroundings.
Monte Altissimo: For experienced paragliders looking for a more demanding flight.

Types of Paragliding:
Tandem Flights: With a trained instructor are provided to people who have no prior paragliding experience.
Solo Flights: Experienced paragliders can enjoy the pleasure of flying solo.

Important Considerations:
Paragliding is heavily reliant on wind conditions. It is critical to verify weather forecasts before your journey.
Safety: Always select a reputable paragliding school or operator. Wear suitable gear and follow the safety guidelines.
Physical Fitness: While not exceedingly difficult, take-off requires a respectable degree of fitness.

Paragliding schools normally supply all of the essential equipment.

Cost
The cost of a paragliding adventure varies according to the kind of flight (tandem or solo), duration, and paragliding school. It is recommended to examine the rates and services provided by various providers.

Additional Tips:
Capture the Moment: Bring a camera to document the beautiful vistas.
Respect Nature: Paragliding has an environmental impact. Be aware of your surroundings and follow instructions.
Local Regulations: Familiarize yourself with local rules and permissions, as needed.

Soaring above Lake Garda is a unique experience that will leave you with cherished memories. You may fully enjoy this exhilarating experience if you plan ahead of time and follow all safety recommendations.

Wellness and Relaxation

The Best Beaches For Swimming and Sunbathing on Lake Garda.

Lake Garda has a variety of beaches to suit different preferences. Here are some of the greatest places to swim and sunbathe:

Beach Types

Sandy Beaches: While not as prevalent as in other Mediterranean destinations, Lake Garda does have a few sandy portions. These are generally popular with families.

Pebble Beaches: The most prevalent type of beach on Lake Garda, pebble beaches provide clean water and often breathtaking vistas.

Lido Beaches: These are furnished with loungers, umbrellas, and, in many cases, cafés and restaurants, making for a more opulent experience.

Popular Beach Destinations

Lazise: Known for its long sandy beach, which is ideal for families with children.

Sirmione: Has a combination of pebble beaches and Lido areas, with Jamaica Beach being a popular option.

Riva del Garda: home to Spiaggia Sabbioni, a pebble beach with a vast grassy space perfect for sunbathing.

Bardolino: Boasts Lido Mirabello, which combines pebble coves and a lido area.

Malcesine: Has a range of beaches, ranging from pebble coasts to grassy regions, to suit to diverse tastes.

The Best Time to Visit

During Peak Season (June-August): When the weather is nice and the beaches are busiest. Expect increased rates for lodging and beach services.

Shoulder seasons (May, September, and October): Provide excellent weather, less crowds, and sometimes reduced pricing.

Winter: While not ideal for swimming, some people like the peacefulness of the lake during this season.

Costs

Beach Access: Most beaches are free to enter.

Sunbeds and umbrellas may normally be rented for a charge at Lido beaches.

Water Sports: Activities such as paddleboarding and kayaking sometimes need rental costs.

Food and Drinks: Beachfront bars and restaurants provide a variety of food and beverage options at differing prices.

Estimated costs:

Sunbed and Umbrella Rental Costs: €15-€25 per day.

Paddleboard Rental: €20 to €30 per hour.

Lunch at a Coastal Restaurant: €20 to €40 per person.

Additional Tips:

Beach Equipment: Bring a beach towel, sunscreen, and a hat.

Water Shoes: Might be handy on pebble beaches.

Respect the Environment: Avoid littering and follow local restrictions.

Check the water quality: While the water quality is normally fine, it is recommended that you check for updates before going swimming.

By carefully evaluating your interests and the time of year, you may select the ideal beach to enjoy the sun and water on Lake Garda.

Local Events and Festivals

Garda Jazz Festival

The Garda Jazz Festival is a lively celebration of jazz music set against the picturesque background of Lake Garda. This yearly festival transforms the region into a musical hotspot, drawing jazz fans from all over the world.

What To Expect

Diverse Schedule: The festival's schedule includes both known jazz luminaries and new talents. Expect a combination of traditional and current jazz genres.

Multiple Venues: Concerts are held in a variety of venues, including open-air stages and intimate jazz clubs.

Festive Atmosphere: The event fosters a vibrant and inviting environment, with opportunity to connect with other jazz enthusiasts.

Local flavors: Explore the lovely villages and savor great Italian food to fully immerse yourself in local culture.

Do's:

Plan beforehand. Book your hotel and festival tickets in advance, especially during peak season.

Dress comfortably: The weather might be unpredictable, so bring layers.

Explore the Area: Seize the opportunity to experience the splendor of Lake Garda and its neighboring villages.

Savor the Local Cuisine: Enjoy great Italian cuisine and wine.

Respect the Environment: Be careful of the environment and appropriately dispose of rubbish.

Don't

Arrive Late: Arrive early to see your favorite acts.

Disturb Other Attendees: Respect other festival-goers by refraining from loud talks during performances.

Leave Valuables: Unattended: Keep a watch on your possessions and avoid carrying significant sums of money.

Drink and Drive: Enjoy the event responsibly and refrain from driving under the influence of alcohol.

Additional Tips:

Bring a Blanket or Chair: For outdoor performances, you should bring a comfortable seat.

Ear Plugs: If you are sensitive to loud noises, earplugs may be useful.

Camera: Capture the festival's amazing moments.

Embrace the Experience: Take in the music and the celebratory mood.

The Garda Jazz Festival provides a unique chance to mix your passion of music with the grandeur of Lake Garda. With careful planning and an open mind, you will have an incredible experience.

Olive and Wine Harvest Festivals in Italy.

Italy, known for its gastronomic legacy, hosts a profusion of events to commemorate the harvest of its two most recognizable products: olives and grapes.

Olive Harvest Festivals

Timing: Typically occurs between late October and early December.

Tuscany, Umbria, Puglia, and Liguria are particularly notable regions.

Highlights include olive pressing demonstrations, tastings of fresh - oil, local food, and cultural acts.

Do's:

Dress comfortably for outdoor activities, carry a camera to document the experience, and talk to locals about olive cultivation.

Don'ts:
Remember to carry sunscreen and a hat, especially if coming during the warmer fall months. Avoid littering and respect the environment.

Costs: Some events may need an entrance fee, while many are free. Expect to pay for meals and beverages.

Wine Harvest Festivals in Vendemmia

Timing: Typically take place in September and October, however timing may vary by area.

Regions: Tuscany, Piedmont, Veneto, and Puglia are famed for their wine production.

Highlights: Include grape-stomping, wine tastings, traditional music and dancing, and local food.

Do's: Dress comfortably for outdoor activities, carry a reusable water bottle, and learn about the many wine types.

Don'ts: Limit your alcohol consumption and respect local norms and traditions.

Costs: Some events may need an entrance fee, while many are free. Expect to pay for wine tastings and snacks.

Types of Wine and Olive Oil

Wine: Italy produces a wide variety of wines, including Chianti (Tuscany), Barolo and Barbaresco (Piedmont), Valpolicella (Veneto), and Aglianico (Puglia).

Olive Oil: Extra virgin olive oil is the most valuable commodity. Each location has its own unique taste profile.

Costs

Entrance costs might range from free to €10–20 per person.

Food and Drinks: Expect to pay €20-€50 per person for food and wine sampling.

Accommodation: Prices vary by geography and time of year.

Note: Please keep in mind that these are only estimates; real expenses may vary.

Additional Tips:

Combine Your Visit With the Following Activities: Many wine and olive-producing regions have beautiful scenery, historic villages, and other attractions.

Book Your Accommodations Ahead of Time: Accommodations can fill up rapidly, especially during the peak harvest season.

Respect the Local Traditions: Immerse yourself in the local culture and relish the festive mood.

Attending an olive or wine harvest festival will help you appreciate Italy's rich culinary heritage while also creating unforgettable memories.

Christmas Markets and Winter Celebrations in Italy.

During the Christmas season, Italy becomes a magnificent wonderland, complete with attractive markets, festive decorations, and traditional events.

Best Christmas Markets: Rome: Piazza Navona has a lively market with homemade handicrafts, nativity figures, and street entertainers.

Florence: Piazza Santa Croce is filled with wooden huts offering local goods, decorations, and delectable food.

Verona: Bolzano's Christmas market, situated in the Dolomites, offers a classic Alpine ambiance with wooden chalets and seasonal decorations.

Bolzano: Merano's Christmas market is a hidden treasure in South Tyrol, offering high-quality merchandise and an exquisite atmosphere.

What To Expect

Festival Atmosphere: Enjoy the magical environment of glittering lights, Christmas music, and the scent of roasted chestnuts.

Local Crafts: Discover one-of-a-kind handcrafted items such as pottery, wood carvings, fabrics, and jewelry.

Culinary Delights: Enjoy classic Christmas delights such as panettone, pandoro, and hot chocolate.

Live Entertainment: Enjoy Christmas songs, concerts, and street acts.

Ice Skating Rinks: Many Christmas markets include ice skating rinks for family entertainment.

Costs

Entrance: Most Christmas markets are free to enter.

Purchases: Prices vary per item, but there are possibilities for all budgets. Food and **Drinks:** Traditional Christmas snacks and warm beverages are reasonably priced.

Additional Tips:

Dress Warmly: Pack warm clothes, especially if you're traveling northern Italy.

Bring Cash: Some businesses may not take credit cards.

Plan Ahead: Check the market's dates and hours in advance.

Enjoy the Experience: Immerse yourself in the festive atmosphere and experience the magic of the season.

Winter Celebrations Beyond the Markets

Live Nativity Scenes: Many towns and villages use live actors dressed in traditional costumes to recreate Jesus' birth.

Christmas Eve Dinner: Enjoy a traditional Italian feast with fish and festive desserts.

Epiphany (January 6th): Celebrate the arrival of the Three Wise Men with parades and gifts for the children.

Italy's Christmas season provides a truly magical experience. Exploring the charming Christmas markets and participating in local traditions will provide you with unforgettable memories.

Chapter 5:

Lake Garda's Culinary Delights

Influences on the Lake Garda Cuisine

Lake Garda cuisine is a delicious combination of Alpine and Mediterranean tastes that reflect the region's unique geographical situation.

Alpine influences

substantial Foods: The hilly north of the lake has impacted the inclusion of substantial foods like as polenta, a cornmeal porridge that is frequently served with game or mushrooms.

Dairy Products: Local cheeses such as Asiago and Grana Padano reflect the Alpine cheesemaking tradition.

Simplicity: Alpine cuisine stresses fresh, basic ingredients, reflecting alpine living.

Mediterranean Influences

Seafood: Because of its proximity to the Mediterranean, the southern side of the lake provides a wide range of fresh fish dishes.

Olive Oil: Abundant olive orchards generate high-quality olive oil, which is a mainstay in many local dishes.

Citrus Fruits: Lemons and oranges are commonly used in both sweet and savory cuisines, reflecting the

Mediterranean environment.
Pasta is a staple of Italian cuisine and comes in a variety of forms, including fresh handmade pasta and dried versions.

Other influences
Austrian and German: The region's cuisine reflects its historical links with Austria and Germany. Dishes include strudel and dumplings.
Venetian: Venice's influence is seen in the usage of seafood and the emphasis on fresh ingredients.

A Unique Culinary Identity
The mixture of these influences has resulted in a distinctive Lake Garda cuisine. Dishes are frequently distinguished by their freshness, simplicity, and utilization of local ingredients.

Must-Try Dishes

Bigoli con le Sarde: A Venetian Classic.
Bigoli con le sarde is a traditional Venetian dish that highlights the region's culinary history. This substantial pasta meal includes thick, hand-made bigoli noodles swirled in a delicious sauce prepared with sardines, onions, pine nuts, raisins, and saffron.

Key Ingredients and Flavors

Bigoli: These thick, rough-textured spaghetti noodles are fundamental to the meal, serving as the ideal basis for the rich sauce. Their texture helps them stick to the savory sauce.

Sardines: The star of the show, adding a salty, umami-rich taste to the meal. They are usually cured and desalted before usage.

Onions: Caramelized onions bring sweetness, depth, and a hint of richness to the sauce.

Pine Nuts: These add a nutty crunch and a unique taste.

Raisins provide a surprise sweetness that complements the dish's salty ingredients.

Saffron: This unique spice gives the sauce a vivid golden color and a subtle flowery scent.

Garlic and Chili Pepper: These are optional additions that give richness and depth to the sauce, depending on your level of heat tolerance.

White Wine: Used to deglaze the pan and provide depth of flavor to the sauce.

Fresh Parsley: Adds a fresh, herbal touch to the meal.

The Perfect Pairing

To truly enjoy the flavors of Bigoli con le Sarde, try it with a crisp, dry white wine from the Veneto area, such as Soave or Verdicchio. The wine's acidity will cut through the sauce's richness, improving the overall flavor experience.

Risotto al tartufo: A Symphony of Flavors

Risotto al Tartufo, often known as truffle risotto, is a culinary masterpiece that highlights the unique flavor of this rare and highly treasured item. It's a meal that requires the best ingredients and thorough preparation.

Understanding truffles

Truffles are subterranean fungus that provide a rich, earthy, and musky fragrance. They are regarded as one of the world's most costly and sought-after ingredients.

The White Truffle: Which is mostly found in Italy's Piedmont area, is regarded as the king of truffles. It has a subtle, aromatic scent and a full, nuanced taste.

Black Truffles: These are less costly than white truffles and have a gentler, earthier flavor.

Key Ingredients in Risotto al Tartufo

Arborio Rice: This short-grain Italian rice is important for achieving the creamy texture of risotto. Its high starch content releases after cooking, giving in a rich, creamy texture.

Truffle: The star of the meal, whether white or black, should be freshly grated over the risotto right before serving.

Broth: To cook the rice, use a tasty vegetable or meat broth, which adds depth and richness.

Butter and Parmesan Cheese: These are give the risotto a luscious texture

Onion and Garlic: Provide as a foundation for the risotto's taste character.

White Wine: Deglazes the pan while also adding depth to the meal.

The Art of Risotto Risotto requires regular stirring to obtain the desired creamy texture. The rice should be toasted in butter and onion before gently adding the broth, one ladleful at a time, allowing each addition to soak before adding another.

The Truffle Experience

The real magic of risotto al tartufo occurs at the end. Freshly grated truffle is shaved over the completed risotto to release its captivating scent and taste. The contrast between the creamy rice and the pungent truffle is definitely remarkable.

Pairing with Wine

A glass of white wine, such as Piedmontese Barbera or Langhe Nebbiolo, might balance the richness of the truffle risotto.

Polenta with Osèi: A Sweet Surprise.

Contrary to its name, Polenta e Osèi (Polenta and Birds) is a lovely sweet delicacy from Bergamo, Italy. This dish showcases the region's rich pastry-making culture.

A Misleading Name.
Although the name suggests a big, savory dinner, this pastry is far from that. In this example, "polenta" alludes to the cake's design, which resembles a mound of polenta, and "osèi" (birds) are small chocolate or marzipan birds perched on top.

The Sweet Composition

Sponge Cake: The dessert's basis is a light and airy sponge cake, creating a delicate and moist texture.

Cream Filling: A rich and creamy filling, usually prepared with chocolate, butter, and hazelnuts, is sandwiched between the sponge cakes.

Marzipan: A thick coating of marzipan coats the cake, giving it its signature golden hue.

Chocolate Birds: The cake's top is decorated with small chocolate birds, which are generally constructed of marzipan coated in chocolate.

Origins and Significance
Polenta e Osèi is an integral part of Bergamo's culinary tradition. The actual roots of the term are unknown,

however it is said to have arisen from the cake's form and ornamental birds. This dish represents the region's pastry-making expertise and is regarded as a local treasure.

Dining Recommendations

Discover the Best Restaurants in Sirmione, Malcesine, and Beyond.
Lake Garda has a diverse culinary scene to suit all tastes and budgets. Here are some of the best-rated restaurants in Sirmione, Malcesine, and beyond, along with information on their specialties, ambiance, and pricing.

Sirmione
Ristorante Grotta di Dosso offers a unique blend of traditional and contemporary food. The breathtaking lake views enhance the wonderful cuisine. Expect to spend between €80 to 120 per person.

- **Specialties:** Include fresh seafood, pasta meals, and local wines.
- **Ambiance:** Upscale and romantic, with stunning vistas.
- **Best Time to Visit:** In the summer, evenings are ideal for a romantic meal or lunch on the outside patio.

La Taverna del Pescatore: Seafood aficionados will enjoy the restaurant's fresh catch. The cozy setting and polite service improve the eating experience. Expect to spend between €50 to 80 per person.

- **Specialties:** Include various seafood dishes, grilled fish, and pasta with seafood sauces.
- **Ambiance:** Casual and inviting, with an emphasis on fresh food.
- **Best time to visit:** Any time of day, but especially for supper.

Malcesine

Locanda al Porto: This beautiful restaurant serves traditional local food with a contemporary touch. The spectacular lake views provide a fantastic dining experience. Expect to spend between €60 to 90 per person.

- **Specialties:** Include fresh pasta, grilled meats, and local seafood dishes.
- **Ambiance:** Relaxed and friendly with a hint of elegance.
- **Finest time to go:** Evenings offer the finest vistas, although noon is also nice.

Al Focol: This is a family-run eatery that serves traditional home-cooked meals. The welcoming ambiance and friendly service make it a neighborhood favorite. Expect to pay around €40-60 per person.

- **Specialties:** Include polenta, grilled meats, and substantial soups.

- **Ambiance:** Cozy and easygoing, ideal for a relaxing supper.
- **Best time to go:** Any time of day, particularly for lunch or a casual supper.

Beyond Sirmione and Malcesine.

Restaurant Gardone: Located in Gardone Riviera, this Michelin-starred restaurant provides an exceptional dining experience. Expect to pay around €150-200 per person.

Specialties: Include innovative cuisine made with locally sourced products.

Ambiance: upscale and sophisticated, with exceptional service.

The best vime to visit: This is in the evening for a special event.

Agriturismo Le Carpe: This quaint agriturismo serves true farm-to-table food. Experience fresh, seasonal foods in a rustic atmosphere. Expect to pay around €40-60 per person.

- **Specialties:** Include pasta meals, grilled meats, and local cheeses.
- **Ambiance:** Relaxed and informal, ideal for a casual supper.

- Lunch or supper is the best time to visit, especially during the warmer months when you can enjoy the outside seats.

Tips:
- Make reservations in advance, especially during the high season.
- Consider sharing food to sample different flavors.
- Pair your dinner with local wines to enhance the experience.
- Dress properly for the restaurant's atmosphere.

Exploring Lake Garda's rich food scene will introduce you to a world of sensations and experiences.

Lakeside Cafés & Hidden Culinary Gems in Lake Garda

Lake Garda is more than simply breathtaking scenery and outdoor experiences; it is also a sanctuary for coffee and cuisine enthusiasts. Charming cafés dot the beachfront, serving everything from light appetizers to scrumptious pastries and refreshing beverages.

Relax and Refuel at These Lakeside Cafés in Sirmione.

Jamaica Beach: This famous beach club features a beautiful café with a panoramic lake view. Enjoy cool beverages, light appetizers, and delectable gelato. Expect to pay €15-20 for a modest lunch and beverages.

Bar Gelateria Due Torri: This quaint café serves handmade pastries, gelato, and coffee. Take a seat on the patio and soak in the atmosphere. Expect to pay roughly €5-10 for a coffee and cake.

Malcesine:

Cafe Teatrino: Situated in the center of Malcesine, this café provides an ideal location for breakfast, lunch, or a leisurely coffee. Expect to pay about €10-15 for a modest lunch and beverages.

Bar Belvedere: Perched on a hill overlooking the lake, this café provides spectacular views and a peaceful atmosphere. Enjoy a refreshing drink and a little snack while admiring the view. Expect to pay between €12-18 for a modest lunch and beverages.

Hidden Culinary Gems: Off the Beaten Path Finds

Bardolino: Trattoria al Porto is a beautiful restaurant with a café menu with fresh pastries and great coffee. Enjoy a leisurely breakfast or afternoon tea with a view of the lake. A coffee and pastry will cost around €8-12.

In Limone sul Garda:

Visit Caffè Centrale: A historic café that serves classic Italian pastries and coffee. Immerse yourself in the local culture while savoring a delicious treat. Expect to pay about €5-8 for a coffee and pastry.

Tips for a Perfect Café Experience.
Embrace Slow Pace: Take your time enjoying the ambiance and savoring your coffee or snack.
Try Local Specialties: Many cafés serve local delicacies such as gelato, pastries, and cakes.
People-Watch: Lakeside cafés provide excellent opportunities for people watching.
Support Local Businesses: Choose independent cafes over chain coffee shops to help the local economy.

Exploring the various cafés around Lake Garda will allow you to discover hidden gems and create unforgettable memories.

Wine Tasting and Vineyard Tours at Lake Garda
Lake Garda is known not just for its breathtaking scenery, but also for its great wine production. A wine tasting tour is a fantastic opportunity to discover the region's rich culinary traditions.

Key Wine Regions around Lake Garda
Lugana: This white wine, largely derived from the Turbiana grape, is the star of the Lake Garda show. It is

distinguished by its crisp, refreshing flavor with flowery and fruity undertones.

Bardolino: Well-known for its red wines, but it also produces light-bodied, easy-drinking alternatives that are ideal for summer.

Valpolicella: While not precisely from Lake Garda, Valpolicella wines are popular across the region. Depending on the style, these wines might be light and fruity or deep and robust.

Vineyard Tours & Tastings

Many vineyards provide tours and tastings, allowing visitors to learn about the winemaking process and experience various kinds. Some prominent alternatives are:

Guided Tours: These tours often involve trips to vineyards, cellars, and winemaking facilities, followed by a sample of the winery's offerings.

Self-Guided Tours: Many vineyards have self-guided tours, which allow you to explore at your own speed.

Wine Tasting Events: Some vineyards organize unique events like wine and food pairings or harvest festivals.

Tips for Wine Tasting:

Spit or Swallow: It is permissible to spit away wine when sampling several varietals.

Take Notes: If you're serious about wine, you should take notes on the tastes and smells of each wine.

Pair Wine with Food: Many vineyards provide food pairings to improve the wine tasting experience.

Learn About the Winemaking Process: Understanding the winemaking process might enhance your enjoyment for the wine.

Best time to visit

The fall months, September through November, are perfect for wine tasting since the harvest season is in full gear. However, wine excursions and tastings are provided all year.

Costs

The Costs for wine tours and tastings vary by vineyard and expertise. Expect to spend between €20 and €50 per person for a basic tour and sampling.

A wine tasting trip will allow you to not only enjoy the joys of Lake Garda's wines, but also obtain a better understanding of the region's rich agricultural legacy.

Local Beverages

Garda wines include Chiaretto, Lugana, and Bardolino.

Lake Garda is a wine lover's dream, offering a wide range of outstanding wines that compliment the region's food and breathtaking surroundings. Let's look at three of the most iconic: Chiaretto, Lugana, and Bardolino.

Chiaretto di Bardolino
Style: A light, pleasant rosé wine with a lovely pink tint.
Grapes: Mostly Corvina, Rondinella, and Molinara.
Taste Profile: Fruity scents and tastes with cherry, strawberry, and flowery overtones. It is usually dry and crisp, with a nice acidity.
Food Pairing: Ideal with aperitifs, grilled seafood, salads, and light pasta dishes.

Lugana
Style: A crisp, dry white wine with a pronounced mineral taste.
Grapes: Primarily Turbiana (Trebbiano di Lugana).
Taste Profile: Flavors of white flowers, citrus, and almonds with a crisp, refreshing aftertaste.
Food Pairing: Perfect with shellfish, risotto, and light poultry dishes.

Bardolino
Style: A light-bodied red wine with fruity and easy-drinking qualities.
Grapes: Mostly Corvina, Rondinella, and Molinara.

The Taste Profile: Includes cherry, red berries, and grassy undertones. It's usually medium-bodied, with gentle tannins.
Food Pairing: Goes nicely with pizza, spaghetti, and grilled white meat.

Wine Tasting and Tours

Many vineyards near Lake Garda provide tours and tastings, allowing you to learn about the region's winemaking history while also sampling its exquisite wines. Some popular wine-producing regions are Bardolino, Lugana, and Cavaion Veronese.

Limoncello and Other Local Spirits

Lake Garda, with its abundance of citrus fruits, is well-known for producing limoncello, a delicious lemon liqueur. However, the area produces a wide range of different spirits that represent its rich gastronomic past.

Limoncello, the iconic Lake Garda Liqueur:

Distinct Taste: A sweet and tart liqueur created with lemon zest, sugar, and alcohol.
Best Enjoyed: Traditionally served cold as a digestif following a meal. It may also be used to flavor beverages and sweets.

Production: Traditionally, lemon zest is infused in alcohol for many weeks before being combined with sugar and water.

Variations: Some makers experiment with various citrus fruits, resulting in flavors such as arancello (orange liqueur) and meloncello.

Other Local Spirits.

Grappa: Grappa, a distilled grape pomace brandy, is a famous Italian after-dinner drink. It can be consumed straight, on the rocks, or as a foundation for cocktails.

Amaro: This bitter liquor is typically used after a meal to ease digestion. It contains a combination of herbs, spices, and botanicals.

Fruit-based Liqueurs: In addition to limoncello, the region produces a variety of fruit-based liqueurs such as peach, strawberry, and raspberry.

Where To Try Local Spirits

Many restaurants, taverns, and gelaterias near Lake Garda serve limoncello and other local spirits. You may also visit local distilleries and wineries to try a range of products. Some even provide guided tours and samples.

Tips for Enjoying Local Spirits:

Pairings: Limoncello is commonly served with dessert, whilst grappa and amaro are generally offered after dinner.

Cocktails: Experiment with various drink recipes including local spirits.

Moderation: Consume these alcohol responsibly.

Explore the world of local spirits to enhance your Lake Garda experience and discover new flavors.

Aperitivo Tradition: Lake Garda Style

Lake Garda provides the ideal location for indulging in the Italian custom of aperitivo. With its breathtaking vistas and laid-back environment, the area offers countless possibilities to enjoy this pre-dinner ritual.

What To Expect

Aperitivo is often a gathering of friends or coworkers to share a drink and small snacks before dinner. Lake Garda offers a number of options:

Classic Aperitivo: Enjoy a glass of Aperol Spritz, Campari Spritz, or Negroni with an assortment of olives, crisps, and nuts.

Buffet Style: Many pubs and restaurants serve a buffet with a variety of appetizers, including cold cuts and cheeses, mini pasta meals, and grilled veggies.

Plated Aperitivo: Some restaurants serve a fixed menu of appetizers to accompany your drink.

Best Places to Enjoy Aperitivo on Lake Garda.

Lakeside Bars and Restaurants: Many lakeside venues provide breathtaking views and a calm setting for aperitivo.

Rooftop Bars: For a more refined experience, visit a rooftop bar with panoramic views of the lake.

Wine Bars: Sample local wines and aperitivo nibbles.

Tips for Enjoying Aperitivo.
Aperitivo normally takes place between 6 and 8 p.m.

Food and Drink Pairing: Try different combinations of beverages and snacks to find your perfect fit.

Relax and Socialize: Because aperitivo is a social event, seize the opportunity to talk with friends or locals.

Moderation: Take your aperitivo carefully and avoid overindulging.

By adopting the aperitivo culture, you may enhance your Lake Garda experience while also savoring the Italian lifestyle.

Chapter 6:

Cultural Etiquette and Local Insights

Social Etiquette in Italy:

Italy is recognized for its rich culture and welcoming hospitality. While many Italians are friendly to tourists, knowing some fundamental social etiquette will help you create a good impression and enjoy your vacation even more.

Do's

Dress with respect: Dress appropriately for the occasion in Italy, despite the country's easygoing culture.

Learn simple Italian phrases: A few Italian words may go a long way toward expressing respect and gratitude.

Savor the Pace: Italians frequently value quality time and love unhurried dinners. Embrace the slower pace.

Appreciate Culture: Show an interest in Italian art, history, and food.

Be punctual: Punctuality is important, especially for business meetings or formal events.

Use Your Hands When Speaking: Italians are expressive and frequently make gestures to underline their views.

Enjoy the Food: Italian cuisine is well loved across the world. Take the time to taste each flavor.

Don't
Be Noisy and Boisterous: Italians like a quieter setting.
Touch individuals without their permission: Personal space is crucial.
Cut in Line: The Italians cherish order and justice.
Be Critical of Italian Culture or Food: It is preferable to embrace local customs and cuisine.
Expect Quick Service: Enjoy the slower pace of life and savour the experience.

Dinner Etiquette
Use Cutlery Properly: Italians have special guidelines for handling knives and forks.
Appreciate the Bread: Bread is frequently provided with meals and is supposed to be savored.
Order Water: While tap water is typically safe to drink, bottled water is also readily available.
Savor the Experience: Enjoy the people and conversation just as much as the cuisine.

Following these principles will improve your trip experience in Italy while also respecting the local culture.

Language Tips:

While English is often spoken in tourist regions around Lake Garda, learning a few simple Italian phrases will help you enjoy your trip and demonstrate your respect for the local culture.

Essential Greetings and Politeness
Buongiorno: Good morning!
Buon Pomeriggio: Good afternoon.
Buona Sera: Good evening.
Arrivederci: Goodbye
Per favore: Please
Grazie: Thank you!
Di niente: You are welcome.
Scusi: Excuse me.

Basic Phrases For Travelers
Parlo un po' di italiano: I speak a little Italian.
Non parlo Italiano: I do not speak Italian.
Mi scusi, parla inglese? Excuse me; do you speak English?
Quanto costa? How much does it cost?
Dove è il bagno? Where's the bathroom?
Aiuto! Help!

Dining & Ordering
Ho fame: I am hungry.
Ho sete: I am thirsty.
Il conto, per favore: Please provide the bill.

Voglio una birra: I want a beer.

Voglio un bicchiere d'acqua: I'd like a glass of water.

Voglio del vino rosso/bianco: I want red or white wine.

Additional Tips:

Pronunciation: While flawless pronunciation is not required, making an attempt to say words correctly would be appreciated.

Body Language: Italians are expressive, thus they employ gestures and facial expressions to improve communication.

Learn Numbers: Knowing basic numbers might be useful while ordering food or shopping.

Use a Language App: Download a language study software to improve your vocabulary and pronunciation.

By learning these fundamental words and demonstrating a desire to speak in Italian, you will not only find it easier to manage Lake Garda, but also improve your whole trip experience.

Dress Codes and Fashion Insights

Dress rules vary greatly according on the event, location, and cultural background. While fashion trends change swiftly, some ideas stay timeless. Let's look at diverse dress regulations and fashion insights.

Formal Attire

Black Tie: Events often includes a black tuxedo for males and a long evening gown for women.

White Tie: The most formal dress code requires males to wear a white tuxedo jacket, a black tailcoat, and a white bow tie. Women usually wear full-length evening gowns.

Semi-formal: Attire for males includes dark suits, while ladies can wear cocktail dresses or stylish pieces.

Business Attire.

Business Formal: Men and women wear suits or tailored pieces.

Business Casual: Attire includes dress slacks or skirts, collared shirts, and closed-toe shoes.

Smart Casual: Wear includes chinos, blazers, and blouses that are polished yet casual.

Casual Wear

Casual Chic: Refers to fashionable clothing that combine comfort and fashion.

Athleisure: A style that combines athletic and casual elements and is popular for everyday activities.

Beachwear: Refers to comfortable attire ideal for the beach or pool.

Fashion insights

Personal Style: Show your originality while complying to dress code rules.

Color Coordination: Combine colors and patterns to create a coherent look.

Accessories: Dress up your clothing with well picked accessories.

Fit: Make sure your outfit fits properly for a professional appearance.

Confidence: Wear your attire confidently and stylishly.

Specific Occasions

Weddings: The dress code varies according on the formality.

Funerals: Typically need solemn apparel, such as black or dark hues.

Job Interviews: Dress properly to create a good impression.

Dining Out: Dress for the restaurant's setting.

Remember that fashion is a form of self-expression, and the best-dressed individual is one who is confident and comfortable in their clothing.

Laws and Regulations

Legal Considerations for Tourists

While traveling is often a pleasant experience, it is essential to understand the legal structure of the nation you are visiting in order to avoid any unexpected complications. Here are some important aspects to remember:

Passport and Visa Requirements:
- Ensure that your passport is valid for the duration of your trip.
- Before departing, make sure you understand the visa requirements and collect the essential papers.
- Carry duplicate passports and preserve the original in a secure location.

Laws and Customs
- Respect the local norms and traditions.
- Familiarize oneself with the country's laws, particularly those concerning drugs, alcohol, and public conduct.
- Be mindful of clothing standards and cultural customs.

Photography and Drone Usage
- Be aware of photographing limitations in some locations, such as religious institutions or government buildings.
- Understand drone rules, which differ per nation.
- Respect privacy and do not photograph anyone without their permission.

Consumer Protection

- Be aware of frauds and fraudulent activity.
- Understand your consumer rights, particularly with purchases and returns.
- Keep all receipts and paperwork from any transactions.

Health & Safety

- Follow local health and safety requirements, particularly for food and water.
- Get the appropriate vaccines before your travel.
- Get travel insurance to cover medical emergencies.

Legal Troubles

- If you have legal problems, contact your country's embassy or consulate for help.
- Know the local legal system and your rights.

Do's

- Do research the country's laws and culture before to your travel.
- Carry important papers such as a passport, visa, and travel insurance.
- Be respectful to the local culture and traditions.
- Keep up with current events and travel alerts.

Don'ts

- Don't break local laws or indulge in unlawful activity.

- Use drugs or excessive alcohol.
- Display disrespectful conduct.
- Underestimate the value of travel insurance.

Following these instructions will allow you to enjoy your trip with peace of mind. Remember that it is always a good idea to research the unique rules and regulations of the nation you are going before traveling.

Driving Regulations and Road Safety in Lake Garda

Driving around Lake Garda can be a wonderful experience, with breathtaking scenery and the opportunity to explore at your own speed. To guarantee a safe and comfortable ride, drivers must be knowledgeable of local driving rules and road conditions.

Driving Laws and Regulations

International Driver Permit (IDP): While an IDP is not required for all nationalities, it is strongly advised to obtain one in addition to your national driver's license.

Speed restrictions: Be careful of the speed restrictions, which are displayed in kilometers per hour. Speed cameras are widespread, so follow the established limits.

Seatbelts: All vehicle occupants must use a seatbelt.

kid Seats: Children must be appropriately restrained in kid seats appropriate to their age and weight.

Mobile Phones: Using a mobile phone while driving is totally illegal, even with hands-free technology.

Alcohol Limit: The legal blood alcohol limit is 0.5 g/L.

Headlights: Use dipped headlights during the day.

Toll Roads: Many Italian roadways are toll roads. Make sure you have adequate cash or a toll pass.

Parking: Be aware of parking limitations and avoid parking in illegal locations.

Road Conditions and Safety Tips

Mountain Roads: The roads surrounding Lake Garda can be twisting and narrow, particularly in hilly places. Drive carefully and stay alert of other vehicles.

Traffic: Traffic may be intense, particularly during the high tourist season. Be patient and defensive.

Pedestrians and Bicycles: Share the road with walkers and bikers, and remain mindful of their presence.

Carry a Basic Emergency Kit: Which includes a first-aid kit, warning triangle, and reflective vest.

Insurance: Make sure you have adequate auto insurance coverage.

Dos

Do: Before driving, familiarize yourself with the local traffic rules and regulations.

Do: Drive cautiously and defensively.

Do: Use your headlights during the daytime.

Do: Look for bikes and pedestrians before turning or changing lanes.

Don'ts.
- Do not drive under the influence of alcohol or drugs.
- Do not use your cell phone while driving.
- Do not speed or drive recklessly.
- Do not park illegally or hinder traffic.

Following these principles will allow you to have a safe and responsible driving experience around Lake Garda.

Environmental Protection and Conservation Regulations:

Environmental preservation and conservation are major global challenges. Understanding and following appropriate guidelines is critical for protecting our world.

Key Environmental Principles.

Reduce, Reuse, and Recycle: Minimizing waste is critical. Reduce consumption, reuse products whenever feasible, and recycle stuff to help save resources.

Sustainable Practices: Practice ecologically beneficial practices in your everyday life, such as energy conservation, water efficiency, and responsible consumerism.

Biodiversity Protection: Help safeguard wildlife, plants, and ecosystems. Avoid disrupting natural areas or contributing to deforestation.

Pollution Prevention: Reduce pollution by lowering emissions, disposing of garbage properly, and adopting environmentally friendly items.

Climate Change Mitigation: Help reduce greenhouse gas emissions by choosing sustainable transportation, energy-efficient activities, and responsible consumerism.

Specific Rules and Regulations

Environmental rules differ by country and location. Here are some popular instances.

Trash Management: The proper disposal of trash, which includes recycling, composting, and hazardous waste management.

Water Conservation: Entails using water efficiently, such as gathering rainfall and decreasing water waste.

Wildlife Protection: Entails following wildlife protection regulations, not harming ecosystems, and respecting wildlife.

Land Use Planning: Adhering to zoning restrictions and sustainable land development techniques.

Pollution Control: Adhering to air, water, and soil pollution guidelines.

Environmental Impact Assessment: is the process of evaluating initiatives that may have an impact on the environment.

Dos

Do: Learn more about environmental problems.

Do: Support environmentally friendly businesses and goods.

Participate in community cleanup projects.

Do: Reduce your carbon footprint.

Don'ts.

Do not: litter or pollute the environment.

Do not: waste water or energy.

Do not: disturb wildlife or their habitats.

Additional Considerations:

International Agreements: Countries frequently participate in international treaties to solve global environmental issues.

Government Regulations: National, regional, and municipal governments establish environmental legislation.

Individual Responsibility: Every individual may help to safeguard the environment via their everyday actions.

We can aid future generations by learning and adhering to environmental protection and conservation standards.

Sustainable and Responsible Travel

Tips for Eco-Friendly Tourism on Lake Garda

Lake Garda is a breathtaking natural wonder, and its beauty must be preserved for future generations. Here are some suggestions to help you enjoy your trip while reducing your environmental impact:

Choosing Eco-friendly Accommodations

Eco-certified Establishments: Look for hotels, bed and breakfasts, and campsites that have certifications such as Green Key or the EU Ecolabel. These enterprises follow rigorous environmental guidelines.

Energy Efficiency: Choose lodgings that promote energy efficiency, such as employing renewable energy sources and encouraging water conservation.

Local Materials: Choose locations that use locally sourced materials and employ traditional construction processes.

Sustainable Transportation

Public Transportation: Use the ferry system, buses, and trains to lessen your carbon impact.

Walking and Cycling: Explore the lake's splendor on foot or by bike, taking in the surroundings while also getting some exercise.

Carpooling: If you need to hire a car, try sharing it with other tourists.

Electric Automobiles: Look for car rental companies that provide electric or hybrid vehicles.

Respecting Nature
Stay on Specified Trails: To avoid damaging sensitive habitats or upsetting wildlife.
Leave no Traces: Pack out all of your rubbish, including cigarette butts.
Conserve Water: Be aware of your water consumption, particularly during peak season.
Wildlife observation: Observe wildlife from a safe distance and avoid harming their natural habitats.

Supporting Local Economy
Buy Locally: Choose locally made food and souvenirs to help the community.
Eat Seasonally: Enjoy seasonally appropriate, fresh, local food.
Avoid Single-use Plastics: By using reusable water bottles, shopping bags, and utensils instead.

Reducing Waste:
Bring Reusable Goods: Use your own water bottle, shopping bag, and utensils to save waste.
Recycle: Always dispose of rubbish correctly and recycle wherever feasible.
Mindful Consumption: Avoiding superfluous packaging and selecting items that produce less waste.

Educate Yourself.

Learn About Your Local Environment: Understand the area's distinct ecosystems and difficulties.

Support Conservation Efforts: Donate to groups dedicated to preserving Lake Garda's natural heritage.

Spread Awareness: Share your environmentally friendly experiences with others to encourage responsible travel.

By following these suggestions, you may help to preserve Lake Garda's natural beauty while having an enjoyable and sustainable vacation.

Supporting Local Communities and Businesses

Supporting local communities and companies is critical to promoting economic growth, maintaining cultural heritage, and creating a vibrant environment. Here are several useful methods to contribute:

Direct Support.write

Shop Small: Rather than purchasing products and services from giant corporations, prioritize small businesses. This keeps money moving in the neighborhood.

Dine Out: Eating out on a regular basis helps to support local eateries. Explore various cuisines and culinary experiences.

Attend Local Events: Take part in farmers' markets, craft fairs, and neighborhood festivals. These events highlight local items and talents.

Volunteer: Offer your time and skills to local groups or community initiatives.

Word-of-Mouth and Online Promotion

Share positive experiences by recommending local companies to friends, family, and on social media.

Write Reviews: Share your experiences on review sites to help others find local treasures.

Engage with Local Companies: Follow local companies on social media and join their online communities.

Economic Impact

Understand the Multiplier Impact: Recognize that spending locally has a knock-on impact, helping several companies and individuals.

Support Local Initiatives: Help support community development programs like crowdfunding campaigns or business incubators.

Buy Local: To support farmers and producers, prioritize the purchase of locally based items.

Building Relationships

Get to Know Local Business Owners: Making personal contacts promotes a feeling of community and loyalty.

Participate in Community Events: Attend local events to network and support local causes.

Join Local Organizations: Join a chamber of commerce or community group to keep informed and engaged.

Additional Considerations:

Ethical Consumption: Support firms that use sustainable techniques and adhere to fair labor standards.

Diversity and Inclusion: Prioritize businesses that value diversity and inclusiveness.

Long-term Commitment: Actively supporting local communities and companies contributes to a robust and sustainable economy, ensuring their long-term prosperity.

By actively supporting local communities and companies, you help to build a thriving, resilient, and sustainable economy.

Staying in Green Accommodations:

Choosing green accomodation is a great way to lessen your carbon impact while on vacation. This form of hotel focuses on sustainability and minimizing environmental effect.

What to Look for in Green Accommodations.

Eco-Certifications: Look for lodgings with certifications such as LEED, Green Key, and

EarthCheck. These certifications demonstrate a commitment to sustainability.

Energy Efficiency: Properties that use renewable energy, have energy-efficient appliances, and follow energy-saving habits.

Water Conservation: Measures include water-saving fixtures, rainwater harvesting systems, and efficient landscaping.

Waste Reduction: Hotels and lodges that emphasize recycling, composting, and waste reduction.

Local Sourcing: Refers to properties that employ locally sourced food and resources.

Nature Integration: Accommodations that mix in with the natural surroundings and allow visitors to connect with nature.

Cost Considerations:

Green lodgings may offer somewhat higher prices than standard choices. However, the investment typically results in a more comfortable stay since you know you're helping the environment.

Offsetting Costs: Some lodgings have carbon offset programs, which allow visitors to compensate for their trip emissions.

Value for Money: While there may be a charge, green lodgings frequently provide extra facilities and experiences, such as organic soaps, wellness programs, and proximity to nature.

Best Places to Find Green Accommodation
Popular Tourist Destinations: Many major towns and tourist destinations have a variety of green lodging alternatives.
Rural Areas: Eco-lodges, farm stays, and cottages are commonly found in rural areas, offering immersive natural experiences.
Coastal Locations: Beachfront resorts and hotels that incorporate environmental measures are becoming more frequent.

Tips for Choosing Green Accommodations.
Conduct Thorough Research: Visit the property's website to learn more about its sustainable policies.
Read reviews: Check guest reviews to confirm the accommodation's green promises.
Ask Questions: To learn more about the property's environmental activities, contact them directly.
Support Local Initiatives: Select lodgings that help local communities and conservation activities.

By choosing green lodgings, you can help to create a more sustainable future while still having a wonderful and environmentally aware vacation experience.

Chapter 7:

Practical Travel Tips and Advice

Public Transportation

Public transit is a practical and frequently inexpensive way to visit a new location. It provides a distinct viewpoint on local life and culture. Let's look at the numerous kinds of public transportation and their accompanying prices.

Buses

Cost: Buses are the most cost-effective choice, with ticket pricing varied by distance and city.

Coverage: Buses often provide vast coverage, connecting urban and rural regions.

Frequency: Bus timetables might vary greatly. In big cities, buses operate often, although in rural regions, services may be less frequent.

Comfort: Comfort levels might vary depending on the bus type and route. Some buses may be air-conditioned and provide amenities such as Wi-Fi.

Tips: If possible, buy tickets in advance, verify them before you board, and be careful of peak hour traffic.

vessel costs vary based on distance, vessel type, and added services.

Ferries

Cost: Ferry services connect mainland areas to islands or coastal settlements.

Frequency: Ferry timetables vary according on season and demand.

Comfort: Ferry experiences range from simple to opulent, with alternatives for all budgets.

Tips: Reserve ferry tickets in advance, especially during peak season, and pack appropriately for maritime travel.

Trains

Cost: Train costs vary by distance, train type, and ticket class (normal, reduced, or high-speed).

Coverage: Trains often connect large cities and towns, providing long-distance and regional service.

Frequency: Train timetables vary according on route. High-speed trains generally have frequent departures.

Trains provide many levels of comfort, ranging from basic to opulent.

Tips: Buy your tickets ahead of time, especially for long-distance travels, and think about getting rail passes for numerous trips.

Additional Tips:

Public Transit Cards: Many cities give transit cards or tickets that include discounts and convenience.

Timetables and Maps: Prior to your journey, familiarize yourself with public transit timetables and routes.

Language Barriers: Learn some basic words in the local language to help with ticket sales and questions.

Safety: Be careful of your surroundings, particularly when traveling alone at night.

Understanding the various kinds of public transportation and preparing appropriately allows you to have a smooth and cost-effective travel experience.

Renting a Car:

Renting a car might provide you with more flexibility and freedom when visiting a new location. However, it is critical to understand the procedure and potential expenses involved.

Requirements for Renting a Car

Valid Driver's License: Renting a car normally requires a valid driver's license from the country of residency.

Age Restrictions: Most rental agencies require a minimum age of 21 or 25. Drivers under the age of 25 may incur additional costs.

Credit Card: A valid credit card is frequently required for the rental and to settle any fees.

International Driver Permit (IDP): Although not usually required, an IDP can be beneficial in some countries.

Driving Record: Some rental businesses may examine your driving history.

Understanding Rental Costs.

The base Rate: The actual cost of the automobile, which is determined by the car type, rental length, and location.

Insurance: Rental businesses provide a variety of insurance choices, including collision damage waiver (CDW) and liability insurance. Before getting additional insurance, be sure your personal vehicle insurance policy covers the situation.

Additional Expenses: These may include airport surcharges, taxes, fees for additional drivers, and young driver fees.

Gasoline: Some rental businesses provide full-to-full gasoline alternatives, while others utilize a pre-paid fuel system.

Car Inspection and Documentation

Inspect the Car: Before driving away, properly inspect the vehicle for any pre-existing damage and report it to the rental company.

Rental Agreement: Carefully read the rental agreement, including the terms and conditions, insurance coverage, and payment information.

Driving Laws and Regulations

Local regulations: Learn about local traffic regulations, speed restrictions, and road rules.

Seatbelts: Always wear your seatbelt, and make sure your passengers do as well.

kid Seats: When traveling with children, utilize proper kid safety seats.

Mobile Phones: Many nations make it unlawful to use a cell phone while driving.

Returning the Car

Fuel: When returning the car, ensure it has the same quantity of petrol as when you picked it up, unless you choose a pre-paid fuel option.

Inspection: The rental provider will check the automobile for any new damage.

Additional Charges: Prepare for any charges, like as late fees or cleaning fees.

Understanding these essential aspects allows you to hire a car with confidence and have a hassle-free vacation experience.

Biking and Walking:

Exploring a new location on foot or by bike provides a distinct viewpoint and helps you to fully immerse yourself in the local culture. Here's a guide to help you make the most of your hiking and riding trips.

Benefits of Walking and Biking

Health and Wellness: Walking and biking provide several health and wellness benefits. Improves both physical and mental wellness.

Environmental Friendliness: Decreases carbon footprint.

Cost-effective: Frequently free or low-cost transportation.

Intimate Exploration: Enables a closer connection with the destination.

Discovering Secret Gems: Discovers secret nooks and local landmarks.

Essential Gear

Comfortable Shoes: For walking, choose well-fitting, supportive shoes.

Bike Helmet: Required in many countries, and necessary for safety.

A Bike Lock: Protects your bike against theft.

Map or GPS: Find your way around effectively.

Water Bottle: Stay hydrated.

Sunscreen and a Hat: Protect yourself from the sun.

Safety Tips

Plan Your Route: Do your research ahead of time to find safe and picturesque routes.

Be Aware of Surroundings: Stay vigilant and observant of your surroundings.

Traffic Safety: Obey traffic regulations and remain visible to vehicles.

Bike Maintenance: Ensure that your bike is in good functioning order.

Emergency Contact: Inform someone about your plans, especially for longer travels.

Bike Rental
Availability: Bike rentals are widely available in major cities and tourist sites.
Types of Bikes: Select a bike that meets your requirements, such as a city bike, mountain bike, or electric bike.
Cost: Rental fees vary according on bike model and rental time.
Helmet: Most rental businesses include helmets.

Bicycle and Walking Tours
Guided Tours: Consider taking a guided bike or walking tour to learn about the local history and culture.
Self-guided Tours: Using a map or GPS app, you may explore at your own speed.
Combine Walking and Biking: For a more diverse experience, combine both forms of transportation.

Walking and biking can help you have a better, more sustainable, and genuine vacation experience.

Managing Money and Expenses

Currency Exchange and ATM Tips

Managing your money when traveling is critical. Here are some recommendations for currency conversion and ATM use to help you make the most of your money.

Currency Exchange

Research Exchange Rates: Before traveling, research exchange rates to determine the value of your money.

Airport Exchange Bureaus: These are often the least desirable alternative owing to exorbitant fees and bad rates.

Banks and Currency Exchange Offices: Often provide better rates than airports, but may have limited hours of operation.

ATMs: Withdrawing local money from an ATM is typically the most convenient and cost-effective option.

ATM Tips:

Inform Your Bank: Notify your bank about your trip intentions to avoid card blocking.

ATM Fees: Be mindful of any ATM fees levied by your bank or the foreign ATM. Some banks provide fee-free ATM networks.

Security: Use ATMs in well-lit places and protect your PIN when entering it.

Daily Withdrawal Limits: Check your daily withdrawal limit to avoid any unforeseen complications.

Dynamic Currency Conversion (DCC): Always avoid DCC since it frequently leads in poor exchange rates.

Additional Tips:

Carry a Combination of Cash and Cards: It is prudent to have a mix of both for various scenarios.

Credit Card Usage: Although handy, credit card use might result in unexpected costs and currency rate swings.

Emergency Funds: Keep a little sum of cash in a safe place for emergencies.

Negotiate Rates: If you're exchanging big sums of cash, attempt to get a better rate.

Following these guidelines can help you manage your cash properly and prevent needless expenses when traveling.

Using Credit Cards to Manage Your Budget

Credit cards may be effective financial instruments if used carefully. Here is a tutorial to help you handle your money properly.

Benefits of Credit Cards

Rewards: Credit cards provide rewards schemes, including cash back, airline miles, and points.

Purchase Protection: Certain cards offer purchase protection against damage or theft.

Emergency Funds: A credit card might serve as a backup payment option in an emergency.

Building Credit: Using credit cards responsibly might help you improve your credit score.

Managing Your Budget With Credit Cards
Create a Budget: Determine your monthly income and spending to develop a reasonable budget.

Track Your Spending: To avoid overspending, always monitor your credit card usage.

Pay Your Balance in Full: To prevent paying interest, aim to pay off your whole total each month.

Choose the Right Card: Choose a credit card that matches your spending patterns and provides you with valuable incentives.

Avoid Balance Transfers: They are generally associated with hefty fees and interest rates.

Set Spending Limits: Set spending limitations for each category to avoid overspending.

Monitor Your Credit Score: Check your credit score on a regular basis to uncover any difficulties.

Tips for Responsible Credit Cards Use
Pay on Time: To prevent late penalties and credit score loss, always pay your credit card bills on time.

Limit Applications: Applying for several credit cards in a short period of time will harm your credit score.

Read the Fine Print: Know the terms and conditions of your credit card agreement.

Contact Your Bank: If you foresee financial troubles, speak with your credit card company to explore your choices.

By following these principles, you may utilize credit cards as a useful financial tool while staying in control of your spending.

Tipping Etiquette on Lake Garda
Tipping culture in Italy, particularly Lake Garda, differs from many other nations. While not required, a little gratuity is appreciated for excellent service.

General Guidelines
Restaurants: Tipping is not as common as in other nations. A little tip (5-10% of the bill) is appreciated for outstanding service but not required. Often, a service charge is already included in the bill.

In Bars and Cafés: Tipping is not required, however rounding up the amount to the closest euro is standard practice.

Hotels: Tipping is not required, however a little gratuity for room service or baggage help is appreciated.

Taxis: Tipping is optional, however rounding up the fare is standard practice.

Tour Guides: A little gratuity is appreciated for exceptional service.

Additional Tips:

Discretionary: Tipping is entirely at your discretion and is determined by your level of satisfaction with the service provided.

Cash: Small sums of cash are ideal for tipping.

Local Customs: To learn about local customs, observe how people tip.

Remember, the most important thing is to enjoy your vacation and be grateful for the care you get. A simple expression of thanks may go a long way.

Insider Tips for a Memorable Visit

Avoiding Crowds at Popular Attractions.

Enjoying popular places without being swamped by crowds might improve your overall vacation experience. Here are a few strategies:

Timing Your Visit

Early Bird: Arrive at attractions as soon as they open to avoid crowds.

Late Stays: Extend your visit into the evening, when most visitors have departed.

Off-Peak Seasons: Travel during the shoulder seasons for less crowds.

Weekday Visits: Avoid weekends if possible, as they are busier.

Choosing Less Popular Alternatives.

Hidden Gems: Discover lesser-known sites or communities.

Local Perspectives: Ask locals for advice on off-the-beaten-path locations.

Day Trips: Get out of the city and visit surrounding sights with fewer people.

Planning & Preparation

Advance Tickets: Purchase tickets online in advance to avoid long lineups.

Guided Tours: Consider attending a guided tour for a more customized experience and to avoid crowds.

Research: Learn about the most popular times and days to visit sites so you can plan accordingly.

Additional Tips:

Flexibility: Be willing to change your plans dependent on audience size.

Patience: Crowds are unavoidable at certain famous destinations, so keep an easygoing attitude.

Local Transit: Taking public transit might help you avoid traffic.

Off-Peak Hours: Visit sights at less busy hours, such as lunch or early afternoon.

Implementing these tactics will allow you to enjoy famous sights while minimizing crowds.

Budget-Friendly and Free Experiences

Discovering a city or town does not necessarily demand a large expense. There are several free or low-cost activities to enjoy. Here are a few ideas:

Free and Low-Cost Outdoor Activities

Explore Parks and Green Spaces: Many cities offer gorgeous parks that are ideal for picnics, hikes, or just resting.

Hike or Cycle: If you enjoy the outdoors, explore nature trails or bike lanes.

Beach Days: Relax and enjoy the sun, sand, and waves at a nearby beach.

People Watch: Find a busy area and simply observe the world around you.

Free Cultural Experiences

Visit Free Museums and Art Galleries: Many cities have museums that provide free entrance or provide reduced fees.

Attend Free Concerts and Festivals: Check your local listings for free outdoor concerts, street plays, and cultural festivals.

Explore Local Markets: Attend farmers' or flea markets to immerse yourself in local culture.

Library Visits: Include borrowing books, periodicals, or movies, as well as attending free activities at your local library.

Free or Low-Cost Entertainment.
A free walking tour allows you to learn about a city's history and culture.
Picnics: Pack a lunch and choose a lovely location to enjoy it.
Indoor Entertainment: Include board games and puzzles.
Volunteer: Give back to your community while meeting new individuals.
Explore Nature Centers: Many cities have nature centers that provide free exhibitions and trails.

Additional Tips:
Check the Local Event Calendars: Discover free or low-cost activities taking on in your neighborhood.
Use Public Transportation: Save money on transportation by taking buses, trains, or subways.
Cook at Home: Save money on dining out by making meals in your lodging.
Take advantage of free Wi-Fi at cafés, libraries, and public areas.
Explore Your Neighborhood: Find hidden treasures and local attractions in your region.

You may have a rewarding and affordable vacation experience by being creative and resourceful.

Off the Beaten Path Destinations
Escape the masses and immerse yourself in distinct cultures by discovering these lesser-known gems:

Europe
Albania: This is a Balkan country known for its beautiful coastline, historic cities, and kind people.

Bosnia and Herzegovina: Known has a rich history, breathtaking natural beauty, and superb food.

Slovenia: This Alpine nation has magnificent scenery, lovely cities, and great hiking options.

Northern Portugal: Visit the Douro Valley for wine sampling, medieval villages, and breathtaking views.

Asia
Bhutan: Known as the "Land of the Thunder Dragon," Bhutan has stunning scenery, a rich culture, and a focus on happiness.

Laos: This Southeast Asian jewel has breathtaking natural beauty, friendly natives, and a laid-back vibe.

Uzbekistan: Immerse yourself in the Silk Road's history and culture through breathtaking buildings and bustling bazaars.

Georgia: This Caucasian country has diversified scenery, delectable cuisine, and welcoming hospitality.

Africa

Tanzania: Beyond the Serengeti, explore secret beaches, unique wildlife, and a rich cultural legacy.

Namibia: Discover enormous deserts, breathtaking coasts, and unforgettable animal experiences.

Zambia: Visit Victoria Falls, see a variety of wildlife, and learn about true African culture.

Morocco: Beyond Marrakech, discover the Atlas Mountains, Berber communities, and seaside cities.

Americas

Guatemala: Immerse yourself in Mayan culture, visit ancient sites, and enjoy the spectacular natural beauty.

Ecuador: Explore the Amazon jungle, the Galapagos Islands, and the Andes mountains.

Costa Rica: Known for its biodiversity, with beautiful beaches, lush jungles, and a vibrant culture.

Patagonia, Argentina, and Chile: Provide huge vistas, glaciers, and distinctive animals.

Oceania

Fiji Islands: Beyond the major islands, discover hidden treasures with stunning beaches and friendly locals.

South Island of New Zealand: Get away from the throng and explore spectacular fjords, mountains, and glaciers.

Vanuatu: Immerse yourself in island culture, see undersea wonders, and relax on gorgeous beaches.

Before embarking on your vacation, be sure to study visa requirements, travel advisories, and hotel possibilities.

Suggested Itineraries

Suggestions for 3-, 5-, and 7-day itineraries include Lake Garda, Verona, Venice, and Milan.
Let's look at prospective itineraries for various time periods that include Lake Garda, Verona, Venice, and Milan. Remember, these are suggestions that you can tailor to your specific interests and preferences.

3-Day Itinerary for Lake Garda and Verona

Day One: Lake Garda
- Choose a Lake Garda town as your base (popular possibilities include Sirmione, Bardolino, and Desenzano del Garda).
- Explore the town and see local attractions such as castles and historical landmarks.
- Enjoy water activities such as swimming, boating, and windsurfing.
- Savor the local food, which includes fresh fish and pasta dishes.

Day Two: Verona

- Plan a day trip to Verona, a beautiful city known for its Arena and Juliet's House.
- Explore the old center, see the Roman amphitheater, and take a leisurely stroll along the Adige River.
- Consider taking a wine tasting excursion through the adjacent Valpolicella area.

Day Three: Lake Garda

- Relax and unwind at the lake.
- Enjoy water sports or explore the surrounding countryside.
- Visit a local winery for a tasting.
- 5-day itinerary: Lake Garda, Verona, and Venice.

Day 1–2: Lake Garda

- Spend two days exploring the lake, visiting different towns, and doing water activities.
- Consider a boat excursion to see the lake's splendor from a new angle.
- Indulge in local cuisine and wine.

Day Three: Verona

- Immerse yourself in the city's extensive history and culture.
- Visit the Arena di Verona, Juliet's House, and other ancient sites.

- Take a nice evening stroll along the Adige River.

Day Four: Venice
- Take a day trip to Venice to see its distinct appeal.
- Discover St. Mark's Square, the Doge's Palace, and the Rialto Bridge.
- Enjoy a gondola trip across the canals.

Day 5: Verona/Lake Garda
- Choose to stay an extra day in Verona for more exploration or return to Lake Garda for leisure.
- 7-day itinerary: Lake Garda, Verona, Venice, and Milan.

Day 1–3: Lake Garda
- Explore different towns around the lake, such as Sirmione, Bardolino, and Riva del Garda.
- Enjoy water sports, hiking, biking, or simply relaxing by the lake.
- Visit local vineyards and enjoy wonderful meals.

Day Four: Verona
- Immerse yourself in the city's extensive history and culture.
- Visit the Arena di Verona, Juliet's House, and other ancient sites.
- Take a nice evening stroll along the Adige River.

Day Five: Venice
- Discover the city's prominent sights and waterways.
- Explore St. Mark's Square, the Doge's Palace, and the Rialto Bridge.
- Enjoy a gondola trip across the canals.

Day Six: Milan
- Discover the Milan fashion and design scene.
- Visit the Duomo di Milano and the Galleria Vittorio Emanuele II.
- Enjoy a fantastic Milanese meal.

Day 7: Lake Como or Return to Lake Garda
- Take a day excursion to Lake Como for a different lake experience or spend an additional day lounging on Lake Garda.

Customization Tips

Hobbies: Plan your schedule around your hobbies, whether they be history, art, gastronomy, or outdoor activities.

Speed: Customize the route to your own speed, allowing you leisure and spontaneity.

Transportation: Consider employing trains, buses, or rental automobiles to go between places quickly.

Accommodation: Choose from hotels and apartments based on your budget and interests.

Flexibility: Entails being open to new experiences and situations.

To develop a tailored itinerary, conduct research on certain sites, restaurants, and lodgings.

Day trips from Lake Garda

Lake Garda is an ideal location for exploring some of Italy's most famous towns. Let's get into the specifics of these popular day trips.

Verona - The City of Love

Distance: About 100 kilometers from Lake Garda.

Highlights: Include Juliet's balcony, the Arena di Verona, Piazza delle Erbe, and Castelvecchio.

Transportation:

- **Trains:** depart frequently from major Lake Garda towns, making them a convenient and speedy mode of transportation.
- **Bus:** More inexpensive, but typically slower and with less regularity.
- **Rental Cars:** Provide flexibility, but consider traffic and parking.

Cost: Train tickets cost between €10 and €25, depending on the kind of train and the season of year. Bus tickets are usually cheaper.

Tip: To save money, consider purchasing a combination rail and Arena di Verona ticket.

Venice: The Floating City.

Distance: About 150 kilometers from Lake Garda.

Highlights: Include St. Mark's Square, the Doge's Palace, Rialto Bridge, and a gondola ride.are

Transportation:

- **Train:** The most convenient alternative, with frequent departures from Verona.
- **Organized Tours:** Many travel companies provide day tours from Lake Garda to Venice.

Cost: Train tickets can be pricey, particularly during high season. Organized trips are convenient but can be expensive.

Tips: Buy a combination rail and water bus ticket to save time and money.

Milan - Fashion and Culture

Distance: About 200 kilometers from Lake Garda.

Highlights: Include the Duomo di Milano, Galleria Vittorio Emanuele II, La Scala Opera House, and shopping along Via Montenapoleone.

Transportation:

- Trains are the fastest and most comfortable choice.
- Rental cars provide flexibility, but consider traffic and parking.

Cost: Train tickets can be pricey, particularly for high-speed trains.

Tip: To avoid long lines at popular sites, buy tickets in advance.

Additional Tips:

Day Trips vs. Overnight Stays: If you want to truly immerse yourself in the culture of Verona or Venice, consider staying overnight.

Group Tours: Taking a guided tour can give interesting insights while saving time.

Luggage: Pack light for day travels, especially if you'll be utilizing public transit.

Timing: Depart early to make the most of your time at your destination.

By carefully organizing your day visits, you can see the finest of Lake Garda and its neighboring cities.

Customize Your Lake Garda Adventure

Lake Garda has a varied choice of experiences to suit a variety of interests. Let's look deeper at particular activities and concerns for different sorts of tourists.

For Adventure Seekers,

Base Locations: Riva del Garda and Malcesine are ideal base locations due to their closeness to mountains and lakes.

Activities:

- **Hiking and Mountain Biking:** Explore the nearby mountains, including Monte Baldo, with paths suitable for all abilities.
- **Water Sports:** Enjoy water sports such as windsurfing, kiteboarding, sailing, and paddleboarding on the lake.
- **Climbing and Rappelling:** Try rock climbing or rappelling in the neighboring rocks.
- **Outdoor Sports:** Such as canyoning, rafting, and kayaking can provide an adrenaline boost.

Accommodation: Consider staying in hotels or apartments close to your preferred activity area.

Equipment Rental: Many local businesses provide equipment rentals for a variety of outdoor sports.

For Those Interested in Culture and History,

The Base Locations: Sirmione and Verona offer opportunities to explore historical landmarks and learn about local culture.

Activities:

- **By Visiting Historical Sites:** such as castles, Roman ruins, and structures.

- **Art and Museums:** Visit art galleries, museums, and cultural institutions.
- **Food & Wine Tours:** Learn about the region's culinary legacy through wine tastings and cookery workshops.
- **Opera and theater:** Attend live performances at historic places.

Accommodation: Choose hotels or flats in the historic district for convenient access to attractions.

Relaxation and Wellness:

Base Locations: Bardolino and Garda bases provide a more calm atmosphere.

Activities:

- Include spa and wellness treatments at upscale resorts.
- Yoga and meditation lessons might help you achieve inner serenity.
- Relax on the lakefront by sunbathing, swimming, and boating in the tranquil waters.

Accommodation: Consider hotels or resorts that provide spa services and wellness programs.

Cuisine: Concentrate on fresh, healthful foods and regional delicacies.

Family Fun

Base Locations: Lazise and Garda provide family-friendly lodgings and attractions.

Activities:

- **Water Parks:** provide exhilarating thrills and relaxing waterways.
- **Theme Parks:** Explore amusement parks that offer rides and entertainment.
- **Outdoor Activities:** Go bike riding, hiking, or picnicking together.
- **Child-Friendly Beaches:** Relax on sandy beaches and create sandcastles.

Accommodation: Choose hotels or flats that provide family-friendly features such as pools and children's clubs.

Dining: Look for restaurants that provide children's menus and highchairs.

Additional Tips:

Research: Thoroughly investigate your selected activities and places.

Packing: Bring adequate clothing and equipment for your chosen activities.

Budget: Create a budget for your vacation and assign monies to various activities.

Flexibility: Being open to unplanned experiences and unexpected discoveries.

Local Recommendations: Ask locals about hidden treasures and insider recommendations.

By carefully considering your interests and preferences, you may plan an unforgettable Lake Garda vacation.

Final Checklist and Travel Preparation

Important Contact and Emergency Numbers

When visiting Lake Garda, having important contacts and emergency numbers at your fingertips is critical for your safety and convenience. Here's a thorough list to keep you prepared:

Emergency Services (all of Italy)
General Emergency Number (EU-wide): 112.

- This number, which may be contacted in an emergency (police, fire, or medical), is the most crucial to memorize.

Police (carabinieri): 113

- For reporting crimes or emergencies that require police intervention.

Fire Department (Vigili del Fuoco): 115.

- For fire or rescue services.

Medical Emergencies (ambulanza/pronto soccorso): 118

- For emergency medical attention or to summon an ambulance.

Hospitals and Medical Services
Ospedale di Desenzano del Garda:

- **Address:** Via Angelo Fermi, 1, 25015 Desenzano del Garda BS, Italy
- **Phone Number:** +39 030 914 5446

- **Ospedale di Peschiera del Garda (Clinica Pederzoli): Address:** Via Monte Baldo, 24, 37019 Peschiera del Garda VR, Italy
- **Phone Number:** +39 045 644 9111

Ospedale di Arco (near Riva del Garda):
- **Address:** Via Capitelli, 4, 38062 Arco TN, Italy
- **Phone Number:** +39 0464 582 222

Tourist Information Centers
Riva del Garda Tourist Office:
- **Address:** Largo Medaglie d'Oro al Valor Militare, 5, 38066 Riva del Garda TN, Italy
- **Phone Number:** +39 0464 554 444

Sirmione Tourist Office:
- **Address:** Piazza Carducci, 19, 25019 Sirmione BS, Italy
- **Phone:** +39 030 916 245.

Garda Tourist Office:
- **Address:** Piazza Catullo, 1, 37016 Garda VR, Italy
- **Phone:** +39 045 725 6269.

Consulates and Embassy
US Consulate General in Milan:

- **Address:** Via Principe Amedeo, 2/10, 20121 Milano MI, Italy
- **Phone:** +39 02 290 351.

UK Consulate in Milan:
- **Address:** Via San Paolo, 7, 20121 Milano MI, Italy
- **Phone:** +39 02 723-001.

Australian Consulate in Milan:
- **Address:** Via Borgogna, 2, 20122 Milano MI, Italy
- **Phone number:** +39 02 7767 4200

Local Transportation and Taxis
- **Radiotaxi Garda Lake:** (Desenzano and surrounding areas):
- **Phone:** +39 030 912 1021

Taxi Riva del Garda:
- **Phone:** +39 0464 553 111

Train info (Trenitalia):
- **For customer service, call** +39 06 3000.

For Bus Information in the Lake Garda, A.T.V. Verona at
- **Phone:** +39 045 805 7911.

Pharmacies
Farmacia Comunale di Garda:

- **Address:** Piazza Catullo, 4, 37016 Garda VR, Italy
- **Phone number:** +39 045 725 6214

Farmacia Internazionale Sirmione's
- **Address:** Viale G. Marconi, 2, 25019 Sirmione BS, Italy, and their
- **phone number:** +39 030 916 032.

Lost and Found.

Lost and Found Services (Oggetti Smarriti):
- For missing belongings in public locations such as transit hubs, contact local police or the nearest tourist information center.

By keeping this information handy during your vacation, you'll be well-prepared to deal with any problems that may arise while enjoying your time at Lake Garda.

Last-Minute Packing and Preparation Tips

Packing in a hurry might be stressful, but with some preparation, you can guarantee you have everything you need. Here are some important tips:

Packing Essentials

Travel Documents: Passport, visas, tickets, and any other relevant papers.

Essentials: Medications, toiletries, phone chargers, adapters, and travel insurance documentation.

Versatile Clothing: Choose pieces that can be combined and matched to create diverse looks.

Pack Two Pairs of Shoes: one for casual walks and one for formal occasions.

Electronics: Chargers, adapters, and any other equipment that may be required.

Money: Cash, credit cards, and a backup payment plan.

Packing Light

Layer Up: Pack light and layer garments to adapt to changing climates.

Do Laundry: Pack enough clothing for a few days and plan to do laundry while traveling.

Travel-Sized Toiletries: Use travel-size toiletries to conserve space.

Digital Copies: Scan and keep critical papers digitally.

Additional Tips:

Check the Weather: Pack according to the predicted weather conditions.

Emergency Kit: Consider carrying a modest first-aid kit with the necessities.

Packing Cubes: Might help you organize your luggage more efficiently.

Roll Your Clothes: This Save Space and Prevent Wrinkles.

Leave Extra Space: Make room for souvenirs and unexpected purchases.

Following these guidelines can help you pack effectively and avoid forgetting important goods.

What to Do Before Leaving Home

Proper planning before a trip may considerably minimize stress and make the travel go more smoothly. Here are a few crucial tasks:

Home Preparation

Security: Secure doors, windows, and alarms. Consider setting timers for lights to create the illusion of occupancy.

Mail and Deliveries: Arrange for someone to collect mail and newspapers, or temporarily halt delivery.

Plants and Pets: Plan for the upkeep of your plants and pets.

Utilities: Adjust the temperature, switch off superfluous appliances, and notify appropriate providers of your absence.

Travel Documentation

Passport and Visas: Ensure that your passport is valid and that you have the relevant visas for your trip.

Travel Insurance: Purchase comprehensive travel insurance to protect against medical emergencies, trip cancellations, and lost luggage.

Vaccines: Check for mandatory or recommended vaccines and arrange appointments as needed.

Itinerary: Make a complete itinerary that includes travel details, hotel reservations, and scheduled activities.

Financial Preparations

Notify Your Bank: Tell your bank about your trip intentions to avoid card bans.

Currency Exchange: Swap some cash for your destination's currency, but avoid exchanging significant sums at the airport.

ATM Cards: Make sure your ATM cards are enabled for overseas usage.

Budgeting: Create a travel budget to properly manage your spending.

Packaging and Preparation

Packing List: Make a comprehensive packing list to prevent forgetting crucial items.

Luggage: Select appropriate luggage and pack efficiently.

Clothing: Pack flexible, layerable clothes.

Electronics: Bring the appropriate chargers, adapters, and power banks.

Drugs: Include a copy of your prescription with any vital drugs.

Additional Tips:

Backups: Create digital backups of crucial papers including passports and travel insurance.

Emergency Contacts: Before traveling, share your schedule with a trusted friend or family member and conduct research on the customs, culture, and safety standards of your location.

Relaxation: To lessen tension, set aside time to unwind before your journey.

By taking these measures, you may assure a seamless departure and a more pleasurable journey.

Conclusion

Lake Garda, with its breathtaking scenery, rich history, and dynamic culture, provides a wonderful experience for all visitors. Whether you're drawn to its lovely cities, anxious to discover its natural beauties, or simply want to unwind by the sea, this guide is the best travel companion.

Follow the practical advice, suggestions, and recommendations offered to make the most of your visit in this wonderful place. From navigating local traditions and comprehending crucial travel needs to discovering hidden jewels and must-see sights, you're now ready for an unforgettable vacation.

As you begin your journey, keep in mind that Lake Garda is more than simply a location to visit; it is also a destination to appreciate. Take your time seeing its wonders, connecting with its people, and immersing yourself in the unforgettable experiences it has to offer. Your Lake Garda experience awaits—travel safely and enjoy every second of your 2025 holiday!

Printed in Dunstable, United Kingdom

65427283R00077